Savoring the Resurrection

Francis X. Gaeta
Foreword by Joseph F. Girzone

Resurrection Press
Mineola • New York

Lovingly dedicated to
Agnes & Lou
who have been Eucharist to me
for twenty-five years
and to their beautiful daughters
Laura and Rachel,
the joys of my life.

The royalties from this book will be donated to the
Scholarship Fund of
St. Brigid's/Our Lady of Hope Regional School
in memory of
JOHN MURTHA

St. Brigid's/Our Lady of Hope Regional School
101 Maple Avenue
Westbury, New York 11590

Your help to this Scholarship Fund is deeply appreciated.

First published in February, 2000 by Resurrection Press, Ltd.
P.O. Box 248
Williston Park, NY 11596

Copyright © 2000 by Francis X. Gaeta

ISBN 1-878718-58-4
Library of Congress Catalog Card Number 99-75982

Cover design and photo by John Murello.

Printed in Canada.

1 2 3 4 5 6 7 8 9 10

Sequence on Easter Sunday

Let Christians offer praise to the Paschal Victim.
The Lamb of God redeems the sheep:
Christ, the Innocent One, reconciles sinners to the
    Father.
Life and Death struggling in this incredible conflict,
The slain Leader of all the living reigns and lives
    again.
Tell us, Mary, what did you see on the way to the
    Tomb?
I saw the Tomb of the Christ who lives and the glory
    of the Risen One.
I saw the angels who gave witness along with the
    Lord's white burial shroud and face covering.
Christ, my hope, is risen:
He will lead you into Galilee.
Mary, we know that Christ has truly risen from the
    dead.
O great Victor King have mercy on us.
Amen. Alleluia!

Sequentia ~ Dominica Resurrectionis

Victimæ paschali laudes
immolent Christiani.
Agnus redemit oves: Christus
innocens Patri reconciliavit pecatores.
Mors et vita duello conflixere mirando:
dux vitæ mortuus,
regnat vivus.
Dic nobis, Maria,
quid vidisti in via?
Sepulchrum Christi viventis:
et gloriam vidi resurgentis.
Angelicos testes sudarium,
et vestes.
Surrexit Christus spes mea:
præcedet vos in Galilæam.
Scimus Christum surrexisse
a mortuis vere: tu nobis, victor Rex,
Miserere. Amen. Alleluia.

Contents

Foreword

IN OUR FRENETIC SOCIETY it is difficult to find time to pray. It is even more difficult to find time to nourish our inner life with spiritual reading. In many books, it is necessary to spend at least half an hour of meditative reading to digest thoughts and insights that nourish. One of the remarkable phenomenon about Frank Gaeta's writings, especially his latest, *The Great Fifty Days,* is that his daily meditations are like brilliant little gems, which take hardly two minutes to read, but crafted in such a way that the thought stays with you all day, continually nourishes as it offers deeper insights into the life of Jesus and our relationship with him. It is like a timed-release vitamin that stays with you all day long continuing to work within. The reader finds him or herself reflecting back on the readings frequently during the day because the thoughts are expressed with such fresh insights that they capture your imagination and stay with you. Father Frank has done a great service to us all by offering us this latest of his delightful writings.

Joseph F. Girzone

Introduction

MY DEAR FRIENDS,

The Great Fifty Days of Easter are a time for the Church to bask in the sunlight and radiance of the Lord's resurrection while praying for the coming of the Holy Spirit.

The Scriptures of these days contain an abundance of wealth as we reflect upon the presence of the Risen Savior in the life of the apostolic community — the infant Church. In this time the newly baptized pray and reflect upon the new life they have received in the Sacraments of Initiation. The whole Church joins them in celebrating the new life of love that the Lord has given to us through his death and resurrection received in the Easter sacraments.

Following the format of my other seasonal books — *Come Celebrate Jesus!* (Advent) and *What he Did for Love* (Lent) — I encourage you to read the Scriptures for each day, especially the Gospel. Make an appointment for fifteen minutes a day with Jesus. Make the prayerful reading of the Gospel the heart of that time. Allow my reflection for the day to spur your reflection, but do not let me do the work for you. In your heart and emotions write your own reflection. That is your prayer. It is your prayer that is precious to Jesus, not mine. My reflection is meant to help you come to your own precious conversation with Jesus.

Prayer time — our appointment with Jesus — is meant to give us an opportunity, as Fr. Michael Sullivan would say, *"to wallow in God's love."* It is not easy to stick to such a regime of prayer. So many things seem to distract us. I can only assure you that if you are faithful to this daily appointment, Jesus will always be there and your heart and life will change by becoming more and more the heart and life of Jesus.

When you miss days or even weeks of prayers, don't give up on it! Just begin again. The Lord is delighted when you keep your appointment and when you begin again. Discouragement, being down on yourself and being tempted to give up never come from Jesus. Jesus always welcomes us and encourages us to let go of the past and begin again. Your appointment with Jesus will become one of the treasures of your life and you will wonder how you ever lived without it.

In Jesus' love,

THE PASCHAL TRIDUUM

Holy Thursday~The Lord's Supper
Exodus 12:1-8, 11-14, Ps. 116:12-13, 15-16, 17-18,
1 Corinthians 11:23-26
John 13:1-15

THERE IS A MOMENT in the Liturgy of the Mass of the Lord's Last Supper that seems to transcend time and space. It occurs when I remove my chasuble, pour water in a basin, wrap a towel around myself as an apron and begin to wash the feet of my dear parishioners, my dear family, my sisters and brothers — the Body of Christ.

At that blessed moment as I go from apostle to apostle, the Church reminds me what my priesthood is all about. I am called to serve His people, not to be served. I am called to lay down my life in loving service for my dear family.

Once Jesus, the good Rabbi, gave the Apostles His own Body and Blood to be their food and drink, He ordained them and set them apart to serve the community by celebrating the Eucharist until He comes again. To make sure they understood what it would mean to celebrate the Eucharist and to receive the Eucharist, He used an audiovisual aid. He washed their feet.

On Holy Thursday night every Christian is reminded again — powerfully, emotionally and effectively — what it means to be a Eucharistic people. We must be a people who are living the meaning of the Eucharist by our care for one another — especially the poor and the alienated. It also teaches us that if the Eucharist is celebrated without being a pledge of love and service to all, especially the poor, it is empty, meaningless and vain.

At the morning Holy Thursday Mass for our children,

our parents are invited to come forth and wash the feet of their beloved sons and daughters as the clergy assist them. How powerful it is to see our saints, our holy parents, participate in the washing, the total commitment of love that their parenthood truly is. Their beloved children are the Body of Christ, not only at the Washing, but also in the day-in and day-out living of their parenthood. What they do and who they are is holy and precious in God's eyes.

The Church has nothing to give these saints to make them holy. They are holy. They already possess everything. It will be the Church's great joy on Holy Thursday and on every Sunday to remind them of what they already possess — the love and the holiness of the Lord Jesus. The Church will echo to them the words of Jesus: *"Love one another as I have loved you"* (John 15:17).

Good Friday~Passion of the Lord
Isaiah 52:13-53, 12, Psalm 31:2, 6, 12-13, 15-16, 17, 25,
Hebrews 4:14-16; 5:7-9
John 18:1-19:42

AFTER THE READING of the Passion of John and after the sermon, the people of God come two by two to venerate the crucifix. I have a wonderful vantage point at the foot of the cross from which to observe this procession. We use only one crucifix and it is life-size. We encourage our people to take their time and to make this their special moment with Jesus. What a moment it is for all of us as the choir leads us in the touching hymns and chants of the day.

I look out and see throngs of people so respectful and so touched by the drama and the prayer that is taking place. The old and the young are there — children, parents and grandparents — those who are always at church, those who are never at church. Some touch the Corpus, others kiss it and others embrace it — while still others just weep and gently bow. Everyone is deeply sensitive that this is a very special moment to tell Jesus how much we love Him. It is also a moment when people weep for their sins at the cross.

The procession is the March of Life. There's the young woman who had an abortion. Lord, please let this be the time for her to believe in Your love and to begin to forgive herself as You already have. There's the couple who seem to have fallen out of love and are struggling desperately to put the pieces together. Jesus, help them to find their love again. There's the homeless man, the poorest of the poor. I know he's the holiest of all of us, but there's no reaching him, he won't let anyone do anything for him. Lord, I'm so sorry for the times that I resent him coming to me. It's always at the worst possible time. Look, he's crying so hard as he kisses Your feet. Forgive me, Jesus. I'm so sorry.

Lord, there's the woman who's going into the hospital on Monday for tests. She's terrified. She's afraid the cancer is back again. She begs You to let her be OK — just for her kids. She doesn't want them not to have a mother.

Jesus, it seems like the end will never come. They keep coming and coming and coming. Your holy people, Your Living Body, Your Church is together at the foot of Your cross, pouring out all its love and faith and begging You to help us in our own personal crucifixions.

"Dear Jesus, You continue to be crucified in the agony and pain of Your people. Let each of us know today that we do not suffer alone but that You are always at our side. You are our Savior and our friend."

Our Lady of Sorrows

I THINK THE MOST MOVING of all religious images is that of Michelangelo's Pieta. The tender and poignant depiction of the Mother holding in her arms the dead body of her Son has the power to touch everyone's heart. This depiction of Mother and Son is more than a Lenten or even Christian symbol. It is universal in what it depicts and in what it says. While it powerfully depicts the pain, agony, sorrow and desperation of Mary holding her beloved Jesus, it also depicts Mary in her role of every woman, powerfully experiencing the agony and pain of modern woman.

The Pieta is so powerful because it does not depict Mary in glory, but in agony. It does not depict the beautiful and tender image of Mary and Child surrounded by angels and clouds. Rather it presents the other Mary — sitting alone on a dung heap holding her dead Son. No one is there to glorify them or worship them. No one cares if Jesus lives or dies. He's a nobody now. He's a zero. He has no followers, no magic, nothing. If Jesus is a nothing, what about His Mother!

The Pieta is the most moving of all the depictions of Mary. It is so powerful because in it she is totally powerless. Michelangelo is telling us through his art that Mary is one with the poor, the despised, the powerless and the unwanted.

Mary is sister and mother to all the women who wait and suffer with the sons and husbands as they await execution on death row. Just like Mary, they are the only ones there to hold and bury them after their execution.

Mary is the sister and mother of all those women who have suffered abuse and disrespect of all kinds. She is one with all women as they yearn for the respect and rights that they deserve and are so often denied. She is the woman raped and discarded in the former Yugoslavia. She is the child forced into prostitution in the Far East to satisfy the perverse appetites of rich westerners. Mary is the sister and mother of all women who are exiled. She left her country once because of the cruelty and injustice of Herod. Today millions of her daughters — children in arms — are forced to leave their countries and homes, perhaps never to return.

Mary is the sister and mother of the millions of political prisoners, the "disappeared" of Central and South America, the innocent victims of ethnic cleansing and political expediency. Mary is the Rachel of today weeping for her children, but inconsolable because they are no more. Mary is the sister and mother of all those women who have to face unplanned pregnancies. Mary chooses life — the life of this world — and she is there to support her troubled sisters and to tell them that they, too, carry within themselves the Christ Child. Imagine where we would be if Mary had chosen to destroy her child rather than bear Him! Yet, that is what happens when a woman terminates a pregnancy. She is one with her sisters as they make their decisions. She prays that they will choose life, but she loves them and prays for them when they choose another way.

Mary is the sister and mother of women whose children are rejected because of their color, nationality, religion or because they are poor. Mary reminds our society how we must share our gifts with the poor of the world — especially the children. She calls us to peace and a world where children will never suffer the ravages of war or poverty.

Mary is the sister and mother of all humanity. She is "every sister" and "every mother." She is the new Eve. Her role is to be advocate of all, especially the poor and the suffering. All the pain, fear, doubt, anger, loneliness and abandonment that a modern woman may experience, Mary has already experienced. All of the tears that are shed today by women, have already been shed by Mary.

Mary is not the marble statue, clean and neat and tidy, emotionless and asexual, often seen depicted in our churches. Mary is the vulnerable, feeling, passionate woman who is the mother/sister to all modern women, rich or poor, who suffer the pain of life and injustice in our world. Those who suffer the most have in Mary a friend who knows what they are going through and who never ceases praying for them.

It is said that when Michelangelo finished his work, it looked so real that he struck it with his hammer and shouted: "Speak!" This Mary has not stopped speaking to the world. She has not ceased telling us that the Mother of God is not above us or beyond us or even better than we are. What she is still saying to us is that the Mother of God is our mother and our sister and that just as she holds her beloved Jesus in her arms she also holds us and will never let go of us, especially when we are in agony or pain.

Mary is the mother of the political prisoner who was executed for trying to cause a revolution. Could there ever be a bigger "loser," "zero," or "nothing," than the mother of a dead criminal? No one wants to know her or be with her. No one wants to speak to her or look at her. She is despised. She doesn't matter. She's a throwaway. The Mother of God is a throwaway. She suffers everything so that all people — but especially women — will know that she not only understands their pain, but she has gone through it herself. She is not a statue in a safe niche. She is woman.

In the season of Lent we observe Mary as she comforts Jesus in His passion and death. The real tragedy is not that Jesus once suffered, but that He continues to bear the

Passion in His suffering sisters and brothers. Mary is still with Him as she comforts and holds Him in the least of His sisters and brothers. Our call is to bring the Passion to an end by working for justice for all of our sisters and brothers.

As Mary comes to the tomb she knows that the stone has to be rolled away. She also knows that she's not able to do it herself. She believes that somehow the Lord will provide and He will take care of it all — and He does!

Mary's attitude should be a great encouragement for us at Easter. We don't have to do it all ourselves. The Lord is there for us. We can't push the stone away from our hearts all by ourselves. That's why we have a Savior. That's why we have Jesus.

Christianity is not the religion of willpower alone. Christianity is the faith that proclaims that when we are weak, it is then that we are strong. Christianity looks to a Savior who will push the stone with us, not instead of us.

Resurrection faith is the acknowledgment that Jesus lives and that His life is now our life. The Lord calls us to claim our resurrection with and in Him. The Lord reminds us that He is always with us and that in Him all things are possible.

This Easter the Church proclaims the Gospel of Hope — hope for the world and hope for us personally. This Easter the Church calls humanity to heal the wounds of hate and disunity. The resurrection of Christ from the dead is the promise that life and love will always win out over death and hate. In His resurrection Christ rewrites the Book of Genesis. Creation begins again.

Holy Saturday
Isaiah 52:13-53:12

Suffering and Triumph of the Servant of the Lord

TODAY IS THE GREAT SABBATH REST as we await the Lord's resurrection. In our church the statue of the dead Christ lies in
state while confessions are heard. All day long people come
to watch and pray at this holy place. Again our people need
to touch and kiss the statue. The physical and tangible is so
helpful to our prayer and understanding of these holy
events. We wait with Jesus with the knowledge that He will
rise, and our prayer is a prayer of hope and petition begging the Lord that we might also rise again and leave
behind in the tomb all that is dead and decaying, all that
stinks.

As we wait with Jesus we wait in hope, sure that new
life is ours for the asking and that Easter will mean a new
beginning of life and another chance to get it right this time.

In late afternoon many people gather together around
the dead Christ to pray midday prayer. It is our last time
together before the Easter Vigil and the Eucharists of Easter
Day. It is our final moment to prayerfully thank the Lord for
the graces of Lent and Holy Week and for the incredible
grace of having a family in faith to share the events of salvation. For all the beauty and power of these holy days,
what would they all mean without sisters and brothers who
not only believe with us but nourish, increase, and at times,
challenge our faith?

This holy time is the opportunity for the Church to
pass through the paschal mystery. Lent, Holy Week and
Easter are not just times for individuals to be changed and
healed. These days are also meant for the Church itself to

repent of her sins, to beg pardon, to make peace and to confess with all Her heart that Jesus is the only Lord and that we, personally, and as His Church, are His unworthy servants in constant need of reformation and purification.

Personally and institutionally we are called to give up power, abusive authority, lack of faith, materialism and mistrust of God's people and to look to Jesus as the Suffering Servant who comes not to be served, but to serve, and to give His life as ransom for many.

"Christ for our sakes became obedient until death, even death on a Cross, for which God has exalted Him and given Him the name above every other name" (Philippians 2).

The Great Vigil of Easter

Tonight we hear the story of our salvation — the story of God's total love for us from the beginning of time. If you are not able to reflect on all of the readings, I suggest the ones which are highlighted: Genesis 1:1-2:2; Genesis 22:1-18; **Exodus 14:15-15:1***; Isaiah 54:5-14; Isaiah 55:1-11; Baruch 3:9-15, 32-4:4; Ezekiel 36:16-28;* **Romans 6:3-11**
Matthew 28:1-10 *(Cycle A),* **Mark 16:1-8** *(Cycle B),*
Luke 24:1-12 *(Cycle C)*

IF THERE WERE EVER A TIME when the Church pulls out all the stops, it's tonight! The Great Vigil of Easter is a time for God's people to come together and wait or vigil for the dawn for the resurrection of the Lord Jesus Christ.

There are moments in our life when we are called upon to share our heart, all that we are, and all that we know, with someone we love. Moments like that occur when we are at the bedside of someone who is very ill. They occur when a son or daughter is leaving home to go to college, to marry, or for a job transfer. They happen when our children have their own children. They are peak moments of communication when we try to say everything that is in our hearts.

The Easter Vigil is one of those moments. The Church tries to tell her new members who will be baptized and those who will renew their Baptismal vows all she can about Jesus, life and salvation. She does this through signs and symbols like light and darkness, fire and smoke, oil and water, the laying on of hands, and bread and wine. All these elements together attempt to explain the mystery of salvation that we experience in Jesus Christ as we die with Him and rise to a new and glorious life.

The Church tries to put the finishing touches on her new members tonight as she calls them to the waters of Baptism; as she pours the Oil of Gladness over them; as she plunges them forth to a new life of Jesus in the Holy Sacrament of the Eucharist.

In many divine and beautiful ways the Church will explain to them what it means to die to sin and to rise to a new life. The Church will teach them that what they believe in — this new life in Jesus — they will actually experience and live in the sacraments of the Body of Christ. The Church will teach them that they will become part of the Body of Christ, so real and so intense will be their identification with Jesus.

As the community sees its new sisters and brothers pass through this mystery of death and life, each of us will renew our own personal death to sin and resurrection to the New Life in Jesus Christ. We will each say our "Yes" again to Jesus, to life, to hope and to one another.

THE FIRST WEEK OF EASTER

Easter Sunday
Acts 10:34, 37-43, Psalm 118, 1 Corinthians 5:6-8
John 20:1-9

THE WHOLE WORLD REJOICES as our churches are packed with believers today — Jesus is risen from the dead. The throngs of people that are present do believe. Even if many don't come to church during the year, there is that seed of faith in their hearts waiting for the right moment, right place, right moisture to break into life.

This is true of the people at your church this morning, both the regulars and the visitors. We are all waiting for that moment to break into a new life. Isn't this Easter my special invitation to work on my own personal problems and live the new life with Christ? Isn't it time finally to die to what is old and to rise to the new life which He wants me to have in abundance? Each of us has a history and story. Hasn't it been said that every saint has a history and every sinner has a chance? Easter is our big chance to put things right and start again.

Monday of the Octave of Easter
Acts 2:14, 22-32, Psalm 16:1-2, 5, 7-8, 9-10, 11
Matthew 28:8-15

JESUS TELLS THE WOMEN not to be afraid. He sends them forth as the first evangelists — those who tell the Good News to others. So many of the disciples of Jesus are women. They continue to tell the Good News in homes, classrooms and in the workplace. Most of the work done for Jesus is done by His women disciples. Without them the Church would come to a grinding halt.

As we pray during this Easter season on the mystery of the Lord's resurrection we must thank the Lord for the special graces and blessings that women have brought to the Church. We must also pray and work that women along with every other group in the Church be afforded their place and their rights.

The Church must be the loudest and most convincing herald of human rights. We who are always preaching about the equality and dignity of all people must be the leaders in exemplifying that doctrine in our own families and communities.

The Lord tells us not to fear. Isn't one of humankind's greatest fears the loss of what is unjustly taken or denied? When we live in social, economic and ethical justice there is no one to fear. When an individual or members of an institution treat others unjustly, they are always afraid because the day will come when the oppressed come forth and demand what is theirs.

When we (the Church) walk in justice we have no one to fear. Our lives are transparent. We hide nothing and we fear nothing because we walk and live with Jesus in the Truth.

What are you afraid of?

Tuesday of the Octave of Easter
Acts 2:36-41, Psalm 33:4-5, 18-19, 20, 22
John 20:11-18

IN TODAY'S TOUCHING GOSPEL it is very clear how much Mary Magdalene loved Jesus and how He loved her. It is also clear that what moved and formed Mary, Peter, John and the other disciples was not what Jesus taught them, but how Jesus loved them.

The ministry of Jesus was not about organizational and communication techniques. Jesus teaches everything by His loving relationships. Men and women who are called to preach the Good News have fallen in love with Love. They are so filled with excitement and joy over the love that they have found in Jesus Christ that they have no alternative but to share the gift that has been given to them.

Modern evangelization fails when it becomes too programmed without enough heart and feeling. Almost every convert and anyone who returns to the Church does so because someone in their life loved them, not because of some great scriptural or theological insight. People are mostly hugged into the Church. They are not moved by convincing arguments but by loving witness.

When Jesus calls Mary by her name He says her name in such a way that she knows that Jesus sees every part of her heart and her being. He knows her past, her failures, her broken promises, her yearnings and her hopes. He knows the good and the bad and He loves her just as she is.

As you pray now, allow Jesus to say the most beautiful word in the whole world — your name. Let Him say it over and over, slowly, as no one else ever has. As He does so, realize that He knows you through and through, and that He loves you just as you are and that He believes in you now and always. Your name is a prayer on the lips of Jesus.

Wednesday of the Octave of Easter
Acts 3:1-10, Psalm 105:1-2, 3-4, 6-7, 8-9
Luke 24:13-35

I HAVE OFTEN USED THIS GOSPEL in the funerals of people I consider to be saints. It is after all the saints who really recognize Jesus and see Jesus in the Eucharist. They have a profound faith in the presence of the Lord Jesus in the Breaking of the Bread.

But the saint realizes that it takes more than bread and wine to have Eucharist. For the holy man and woman, all of life is Eucharist, and all that they do — every relationship they live is an occasion to see the Lord Jesus Christ and to share Him.

The Breaking of the Bread begins at the Eucharist but does not end there. Jesus is present in all moments and in all people. Jesus is experienced in all of life and love. The true Breaking of the Bread is living life with faith, passion, joy and love — experiencing the risen Lord in every moment of our lives — even in our sins. In our sinfulness we allow the Lord to take our hand and lift us up so that we may begin again with more humanity and humility.

As we live the Eucharist we become the bread that is broken and we become the wine of love that is poured out upon the earth. We become one in the sacrifice of Jesus as we give our lives for the salvation of all people.

The saints are the body and blood of Jesus. When one encounters the man or woman in love with Jesus, one truly receives Communion and becomes one with Jesus in His loving death and resurrection. Do you recognize Jesus in the Eucharist of your life and love?

Thursday of the Octave of Easter
Acts 3:11-26, Psalm 8:2, 5, 6-7, 8-9
Luke 24:35-48

IN TODAY'S GOSPEL Jesus speaks His shalom to his disciples. They are so upset and confused that Jesus has to prove Who He is to them by showing them His wounds. Jesus is recognized as the Lord and Savior because of the nail marks on His hands and feet. The marks are the proof.

Isn't that still true? How do we really know the disciples of Jesus? We don't judge by fancy words and promises. We don't judge by beautiful churches and successful programs and enterprises. Ultimately, we judge by the marks on the hands of those who are His disciples. We only believe those whose hands have been pierced by the labor of love and faith. We believe in parents who have laid down their lives in love for us. We believe in clergy and nuns whose lives are living the life of Jesus as they lay down their lives like the Good Shepherd did for His flock.

Words are so cheap and easy. Promises are meaningless. What matters is the hard and dedicated work of those whose beautiful hands have been pierced by the love of the Lamb of God in service to His beloved sheep.

Look at your hands. What a prayer they can be for you. Are they pierced by your loving and hard work for your flock? Are they the beautiful tools that Jesus uses to build the kingdom?

Our hands must be like His. They must be pierced by the life of love and service that we live. The wounds, and only the wounds, prove that we belong to Jesus.

Friday of the Octave of Easter
Acts 4:1-12, Psalm 118:1-2, 4, 22-24, 25-27
John 21:1-14

One HUNDRED AND FIFTY-THREE FISH in Peter's net and the net doesn't tear! Is that an image of the Church! Perfect!

But look at the net. It doesn't hold the same kind of fish. They are all different. They are all different sizes, shapes and smells. There are no two alike! The net of Peter

— the Church — is messy, smelly, uncontrollable, but oh, how beautiful! Jesus calls such strange and different types to be in His Church. The best part about it is: we all belong and we all have a special place that no one else can take.

Jesus loves them all — big and small, brilliant and dull, clergy, religious and lay people, saints and sinners, conservatives and liberals, homosexuals and heterosexuals. Singles, divorced, happily married, not-so-happily married, separated, single parents, celibates — we're all there. We're there to support one another, to love one another and to realize that the mercy of our God is beyond our wildest imagining.

The Church is always messy. Rules can never cover everything. They never did — even for Jesus, especially for Jesus. People are what matter, not laws. The Church is called to be the sacrament of God's mercy in this world shouting the healing words of the Gospel: *everyone is a precious child of God, everyone belongs.*

You're a special kind of fish. No one is quite like you. You are loved by the Lord in a unique and special way. Your size, shape, and smell delight Him! You have a special place in His net that belongs to nobody else. Do you believe in your uniqueness the way the Lord does? Do you accept everyone else's?

Saturday of the Octave of Easter
Acts 4:13-21, Psalm 118:1, 14-15, 16-18, 19-21
Mark 16:9-15

THE GOSPEL TELLS US TODAY that after the Resurrection, Jesus first appeared to Mary Magdalene. It adds the interesting detail that he had previously cast seven demons out of her! Wow! Can you top that?

Mary Magdalene had been a prostitute. Jesus changed her life and her heart. He did not do it by quoting and explaining the sixth commandment. Jesus changed Mary by loving her. That love enabled Mary to begin to love herself and thus to leave behind a life that was destructive to her beauty and worth as a human being.

Jesus did not lecture Mary on how her sins hurt God — because they don't hurt God. They hurt us and they hurt the whole Church, just as our goodness blesses the Whole Church and us. Jesus, by loving this woman who had been treated as a thing all her life (probably beginning with a family member who abused her), called her to a new life based on her own goodness and value as a child of God.

Real moral living is not just obeying rules, but rather living in accordance with who I am — a son or daughter of God.

The saving moment came in Mary's life when she believed that Jesus did love her and she took his hand. That is the saving moment in our lives, too.

We do not know if Mary ever sinned again. But if she did, she knew there was someone who really loved her and would take her hand again. She knew that she could begin all over again.

So do we. We all struggle with lust, pride, anger, the need for power, addictions, etc. If we're honest we know that we struggle and sin all through our lives. We are all so human — so beautiful. Our holiness is not in being perfect. No one is perfect. We're all struggling sinners. Our holiness is believing in his love and taking His hand and starting all over again. A saint is a sinner who never gives up. Aren't we all very much like Mary Magdalene?

THE SECOND WEEK OF EASTER

Second Sunday of Easter
John 20:19-31 (Cycle A, B and C)

THOMAS, THE UNBELIEVER, is the center of today's Gospel. He cannot accept the reality of the Lord's resurrection on the word of another. He needs to see and touch the wounds of Jesus in order to become a believer. The dilemma of Thomas is our own dilemma.

Faith is a gift. But it is a gift with which we all struggle until we see face-to-face the God of love Who is the object of our faith. Until we see Him we are on a journey. At times that journey is bright and clear and easy. Other times that journey is dark, obscure and difficult.

There are moments in the life of a parish and my own personal life when it is very hard to believe in the God of love. The deaths of young people and children are among the most painful and difficult for me to accept. There are many moments in my faith life when I cry out, "Where is the God of Jesus?" or, "Is there a God?". Don't you do the same?

Our faith is often wrapped in the mantle of doubt. We often struggle with our faith. We make an act of the will that says, "Yes!" but often our hearts are nearly dead with pain and we really don't know or feel anything. Anybody who has truly experienced life will know what it means to believe and not believe at the same time.

I think that Jesus in His agony in the Garden and on the cross was a lot like us in the faith crisis moments of our lives. If we really read the scriptures we see a man who is half crazed with the reality of what the Father asks of Him. Ultimately Jesus will give the Father everything: His faith,

His love, His doubt, His anger and His obedience. We must do the same when the Spirit leads us to those terrible/beautiful moments.

We have a lot in common with Thomas — faith/doubt, side by side. Like Thomas we want to see and touch, but we can't. But there is something very likeable about Thomas. He was honest. In your fighting/struggling faith bouts with the Lord, be honest with Him. He will delight in your honesty and His grace will see you through even if you can't see or touch Him. Think of it: you believe without seeing and touching Him. Your faith is greater than one of the apostles.

Monday of the Second Week of Easter
Acts 4:23-31, Psalm 2:1-3, 4-6, 7-9
John 3:1-8

WHEN JESUS SPEAKS TO NICODEMUS in today's Gospel, He is inviting him to take the "leap of faith" from safe and respectable religion to a new life. Jesus is calling Nicodemus from what is sure and certain to a new reality: the experience of the living God. Jesus is calling and inviting Nicodemus to a life of baptism in the Holy Spirit (See pp. 87-95).

This baptism to which Jesus calls Nicodemus is the giving of one's life to God in the power of the Holy Spirit. It is a new life. Unfortunately this new birth does not happen to most of us at the moment of sacramental celebration in the church. For the most part a seed is planted and a process is begun at baptism, confirmation, ordination, marriage and religious profession.

In God's beautiful plan most of us have to do a lot of living before we become aware of what these graced moments really mean. It is a time in which the Lord touches, blesses and empowers us, but we only come to the full potential of these sacraments after we have lived them with success and failure, grace and sin.

Baptism in the Holy Spirit is one example of what the Holy Spirit is able to do with what we already possess. Prayer groups have ministered to countless numbers of Catholics who were personally led to claim Jesus as their Lord and Savior and invite him to overpower them with His Holy Spirit.

Personally, the charismatic movement empowered me to beg the Spirit to enkindle in my heart the charism given to me in baptism and Holy Orders. It took me years and a great deal of struggling to begin to comprehend the meaning and the beauty of the priesthood — a gift beyond my understanding.

There comes a moment in everyone's life when it is necessary to call down the Holy Spirit upon all that we already possess. Have you begged Jesus to empower and transform your life? your marriage? your relationships? your priesthood?

Tuesday of the Second Week of Easter
Acts 4:32-37, Psalm 93:1, 1-2, 5
John 3:7-15

JESUS AND NICODEMUS continue their dialogue and Jesus challenges Nicodemus and all who are Church leaders. Nicodemus asks how can such a thing like the coming of the Spirit happen. Jesus responds by asking Nicodemus how he can be a leader of Israel and not understand all of this.

Honestly, we are in the same boat as Nicodemus.

Nicodemus was a very good man. He was a Pharisee. He taught the Law, believed it with all his heart and he lived it. He was a just man and a good leader. Jesus called him to something more and greater: to possess the God of love by being filled with the Holy Spirit.

How many times are we as parents, teachers, clergy, religious and lay leaders content to teach the truths of the faith rather than lead our people into a personal and loving relationship with the Lord? We teach prayers, ritual and liturgy, but rarely are our people led to learn how to pray, to speak personally from the heart to the God who dwells within them.

So much of our activity is trying to impart rules, rather than opening our own hearts and those of others to the movement of the Holy Spirit. The real basis of all morality is the awareness of the power and the movement of the Holy Spirit within us. True morality is internal not external.

We confirm classes of adolescents, ordain men to the priesthood, witness marriage vows and religious professions without ever asking people if they know Jesus personally and accept Him as their Lord and Savior. We do not adequately help them to prepare for the coming of the Holy Spirit as we should. We are sometimes very much like Nicodemus — leaders at all levels of Church life who do not understand what these things mean.

Thank God that the modern Church provides many moments that invite people to accept Jesus in a personal rather than institutional way. Thank God for prayer groups, Marriage Encounter, Cursillo, Home Retreats, Ignatian Retreats and all the other means the Lord has used to achieve the new Pentecost.

Have you invited Jesus into your heart yet? Have you been reborn of the Holy Spirit?

Wednesday of the Second Week of Easter
Acts 5:17-26, Psalm 34:2-3, 4-5, 6-7, 8-9
John 3:16-21

JESUS REVEALS TO NICODEMUS the very heart of the Good News: "Yes, God so loved the world that He gave His only Son, so that whoever believes in Him may not die but may have eternal life"(John 3:16).

Today we ask Jesus to send us the Holy Spirit that we might truly believe this Gospel. Imagine God loves you so much that He gave His beloved Son to the world. If we really believed how much God loves us, our lives would be completely transformed. We can never be the same once we begin to know how much we are loved and how precious we are to Him.

Jesus is the flesh and blood expression of the Father's love for us. We look at Jesus and we see the living love of the Father who gives His Son so that we might live. We are so precious and sacred to God that we cannot even begin to describe his love for us. The love of a mother for the child at her breast, the passionate love of man and woman for each other — these are only hints at the power, beauty and passion of the love of the God/Lover for each one of us.

The Son of God freely lays down His life for us. This is love beyond all comprehension. Perhaps the next time that I question "why" or even "if," God loves me this way, I can look at the crucifix and believe in His love for me.

Real transformation, real conversion, takes place when I begin to believe in God's love for me. When I believe in this love, then I can begin to become what God means me to be — a lover like Him, who loves passionately, totally, recklessly and completely.

God is madly, recklessly, passionately and insanely in love with you. Do you believe it yet?

Thursday of the Second Week of Easter
Acts 5:27-33, Psalm 34:2, 9, 17-18, 19-20
John 3:31-36

IN THIS FINAL PART of Jesus' encounter with Nicodemus, Jesus continues to tell Nicodemus about the new life that is available in Him. Nicodemus (like us) is a tough customer to convert because conversion for him (like us) will mean giving up control and power. We seem to prefer a God who is limited and contained by Torah, testament, theology, magisterium and tabernacle. We're used to that kind of God because we've been able to control Him. He can't do us too much harm when we have all the answers.

But the Holy Spirit — that's another story! Nothing is safe when the Spirit is allowed to blow where it will — able to accomplish anything — even Vatican II and Baptism in the Holy Spirit and the conversion of the Churches and Christians, too!

Most of us grew up praying to the Holy Spirit when we needed answers on exams. The Holy Spirit was like a divine computer chip with all the answers. We have matured into a whole new awareness of the Holy Spirit as the very life, passion and love of our God.

Jesus is calling Nicodemus (and us) to a new religious life that's not law or order based. Jesus calls us to a life based on the primacy of love, fidelity and relationships — living in the Spirit and trusting in God's love to guide us.

It doesn't mean that there aren't any more rules, but that the rules are different because they flow from our understanding of who we are — the beloved of God, created by Him a "little less than the angels." Living in the Spirit is not an hour a week adventure, but the total gift of oneself to God's love and following the kiss and the breath of the Holy Spirit wherever it leads.

Believe me. The Holy Spirit is some kisser!

Friday of the Second Week of Easter
Acts 5:34-42, Psalm 27:1, 4, 13-14
John 6:1-15

TODAY'S GOSPEL speaks of one of the great Easter themes —
the Eucharist. In the multiplication of the loaves and the
fishes, Jesus anticipates the days when He will be the food
and life of all through the Eucharist. With all our hearts we
believe that the Eucharist is the Lord Jesus. We must take
the next step: to receive Jesus in the Eucharist means that
we must be willing to be the Eucharist — Jesus in the world.

The thought of being Jesus terrifies us, just as the
thought of feeding thousands terrified the apostles. We say
what they said: "What good is that among so many?"
"What good am I?"

When the five loaves and the two fishes are placed in
the hands of Jesus anything can happen! When we place
ourselves in the hands of Jesus even greater things can
happen.

It doesn't matter how poor, or sinful or limited we
might think we are. Jesus is asking the same thing of all of
us. He is asking us to place ourselves in His hands. He is
asking us to give Him everything we are and everything we
have. We will not be able to be the Eucharist (Jesus) to the
world relying on our own power or goodness. We realize
that we are all incomplete. None of us has the ability or the
holiness to be a good parent, spouse, priest, friend, etc., by
ourselves.

When we give Jesus all that we are, when we place in
His hands our faith, our dreams, our love, our sins, our
sickness, our failure, then He is able to do mighty and glorious things through us. We accomplish miracles in the
hands of the Son of God.

The poorer one is, the more limited, the less gifted, the
more Jesus is able to do. If we get out of His way and let

Him be God, the miracles never stop. What miracles have you performed lately in the hands of Jesus?

Saturday of the Second Week of Easter
Acts 6:1-7, Psalm 33:1-2, 4-5, 18-19
John 6:16-21

IN TODAY'S GOSPEL Jesus gives us a reality check. Giving our lives to Jesus and living in the Spirit does not mean that there will not be stormy days. Like the disciples crossing the Sea of Galilee, there will be plenty of squalls along the way. Our new life is not the promise of a stress-free or problem-free life. It is, however, the promise that Jesus will always be there for us and that no problem or difficulty will ever be greater than the love that Jesus has for us.

"It is I; do not be afraid" (John 6:20). These words of Jesus reassure us and comfort us. He is there in the storm. He is there in our fears, in sickness, in mourning, in unemployment, in temptation and even in sin. Jesus will never leave us alone. He will always be there for us.

He does not promise that there won't be crosses. He does promise us that His grace will be sufficient and that He will get us through anything that oppresses us. Even when the storm rages He holds on to us and He sees us through no matter how frightening it is.

At another time Jesus would say that perfect love casts out all fear. He never said that the things causing fear would be cast out. He promised that the fear would be cast out because love is stronger than fear. Love conquers all. As we grow in this love of our God and our love for one another, our hearts are filled with the Spirit of Jesus. When they are filled with His Spirit there is no room left for fear. *"It is I; do not be afraid"* (John 6:20).

THE THIRD WEEK OF EASTER

DURING THIS WEEK OF EASTER we read from the sixth chapter of John's Gospel. It deals with the promise of the Eucharist that Jesus makes to those who follow Him. The chapter begins with the miracle of the multiplication of the loaves and the fishes. Each day we will reflect on a different theme of the Eucharist suggested by John.

Third Sunday of Easter
Luke 24:13-35 (Cycle A), Luke 24:35-48 (Cycle B),
John 21:1-19 (Cycle C)

IN TODAY'S GOSPEL we find Jesus sharing a meal with His disciples and friends.

Jesus eats and drinks with many people during His ministry. We realize these meals prepare us for the Eucharist. They are also a beautiful outreach to the sinners and the misfits by telling them that everyone belongs at the Table.

Something else is at issue here: Jesus is teaching us how beautiful life is. It is the simple and basic things of life that really mean something.

Consider what it means to have a family and friends who will sit down at table with you and share a meal! Imagine what it means to love and be loved. No matter who we are or what we are, the most important thing in our life is that we are loved.

Jesus was just like us in that. His meals were not things He had to get through. No. His meals were celebrations of love and friendship. Think of the meals He ate with Mary and Joseph and His cousins and friends as He grew up. Think of the meals He ate at the home of Lazarus, Martha and Mary. He was able to relax with them. How delighted He must have been that Martha ignored His instructions and cooked up a storm whenever He showed up. Think of Jesus with the publicans, tax collectors, prostitutes. What meals they must have been! Imagine some of the salty language that slipped out and Jesus giggling over it to Himself.

The first Eucharist took place at the Last Supper, but there were many Eucharistic meals before and after Holy Thursday as Jesus celebrated the sacrament of love and friendship with His friends.

Thank Jesus for the eucharists of love and friendship you celebrate as you sit down and break bread with those who love you. How privileged we are to have people who love us so much they want to break the bread of life and love with us. When we do, Christ is really present.

Monday of the Third Week of Easter
Acts 6:8-15, Psalm 119:23-24, 26-27, 29-30
John 6:22-29

THE CROWDS FOLLOWING JESUS after the great feeding miracle are hungry. They have been fed once and they hope that Jesus will continue this miraculous ministry for their benefit. In their hunger they represent the whole human family, hungry for bread but starving for the Bread of Life.

We are all so hungry for the Word of God. We yearn for love and acceptance. We are looking for meaning and fulfillment, but we often look for love in the wrong places. Jesus assures us that He is the Bread that will give us life.

Jesus welcomes us in our hunger and our yearning to come to Him and feast on the banquet of love. Jesus calls us by name and invites us to take our place at His table and to sup with Him.

As we reflect upon our personal hunger, are we able

to name and admit what we are yearning for? Are we able to give that hunger to Jesus and allow Him to be our Savior? When we come to share in the sacrament, do we come in our poverty, realizing that our emptiness and brokenness are the gifts that we have to give Him? Do we realize that it is OK to be hungry, i.e., broken and empty? Or do we think that the Eucharist is for the wealthy and the healthy?

What a moment of grace it is for us to be able to tell Him that we are hungry and we need Him so much! What a moment it is when we stop trying to manipulate and impress Him with our holiness and our wellbeing!

The Eucharist begins truly to be the Body of Christ when I am able to admit my hunger and give it to the Lord. When I do that, the feast begins and I know that I will never be hungry again.

Tuesday of the Third Week of Easter
Acts 7:51-8:1, Psalm 31:3-4, 6, 7, 8, 17, 21
John 6:30-35

JESUS COMES TO CALL SINNERS. Much of His ministry was table ministry. He ate and drank with anyone who would invite Him. This fellowship with sinners would be a major reason why He would be crucified.

Eating with sinners was more than just having a meal. When Jesus ate with sinners he was saying that He loved them and that He wanted to have communion and intimacy with them. Instead of avoiding them and condemning them, His eating with them said: *"Come closer to Me — you are precious to me. You are my beloved. You belong to me and I belong to you."* It is no wonder that Jesus infuriated the religious folk. He was rewriting the rules. He was also preparing for the great meal, the Eucharist.

Jesus continues to sit down at table with the sinners. He still eats with them. He still delights in telling them how much He loves them. We call that meal the Eucharist or Mass.

The Eucharist is not a reward for being virtuous. The Eucharist is for sinners who come to Jesus asking for His love and help. The Eucharist is the primary sacrament of forgiveness in the Catholic Church. It is true we have another beautiful sacrament in which we celebrate and experience forgiveness, but the Eucharist is the most ancient, the most powerful and the primary experience of forgiveness that we have.

When people sat down with Jesus they experienced the power of His love and friendship and their sins were forgiven. So, too, as we sit down with Him at Table, we are the sinners who are given new life as our sins are forgiven. All of us — modern tax collectors, publicans, prostitutes, misfits, sinners — have found a wonderful table companion — the Lord God, whose love is so great that His delight is to tell us that we are forgiven: *"Say but the word and my soul shall be healed."*

Isn't it sad when the Church tries to decide who is worthy of the Eucharist? Of course, we know that no one is. None of us should be sitting there, but there we are at table — right next to Him! We are there because He has invited us.

Wednesday of the Third Week of Easter
Acts 8:1-8, Psalm 66:1-3, 4-5, 6-7
John 6:35-40

WHEN WE RECEIVE THE EUCHARIST we enter into the mystery of the death of Jesus. The Eucharist continues to offer to the Father the most loving of all prayers — the gift of Jesus on the cross for the redemption of all.

As we share in the Eucharist we are part of the prayer of Jesus. We die with Him to all that is evil so that we might be reborn to a new life in His Spirit. Jesus has called us His disciples, to love one another the way He first loved us. How did He love us? He gave us everything. He gave us His life.

The only true Christian love is that in which we love one another to the point of laying down our lives in love. That is the kind of love husband and wife are called to have for each other. It is the kind of love that brothers and sisters and real friends have for one another. It is a love modeled on that of Jesus in which He gives Himself for His beloved.

When we share in the Eucharist we are saying "yes" to the call that Jesus gives us to love the way He loved — totally and without holding anything back. When we love the Lord and one another like that, then the Eucharist becomes a powerful force for renewal and redemption. Jesus joins our prayer to His to give all glory and honor to the Father.

As we become the new creation, we die to ourselves and rise to the new life of His resurrection. Creation then begins again. Every time we share in the Eucharist we nail to the cross a part of our heart that is not yet redeemed. As we do that our personal redemption begins. What do you need to nail to the cross?

Thursday of the Third Week of Easter
Acts 8:26-40, Psalm 66:8-9, 16-17, 20
John 6:44-51

AS WE SHARE IN THE EUCHARIST we share in the life of Jesus, in His glorious resurrection. In sharing in the Eucharist we enter into the Paschal mystery of Jesus' life, death and resurrection. We believe that the Eucharist draws us into the gift of Jesus to the Father, His death on the cross. In that death we are restored to communion with the Father. We are again made one with Him.

But as we die with Him we rise with Him to a new life. The resurrection of Jesus is our new life as we receive the Eucharist. In the Eucharist, the risen Savior fills us with His life, power and love. We become part of the new creation begun in us in holy baptism and renewed and deepened in the Eucharist.

As we enter the new life in the Eucharist we join Jesus in conquering our sin and brokenness. We sit down with the risen Lord at the holy table and we recognize Him in the Breaking of the Bread. We hear His promise to be with us always, to be our life, and to be our brother and companion.

The risen Jesus is life for us. He is the promise that we will never really die. He is the promise that love will always conquer hate and negativity. He is the assurance that we have overcome all things in His death and resurrection.

In the Eucharist we are reminded that we are to be the disciples of life and love to all people. We are the resurrection of Jesus in the world. We are His life and love experienced in the lives of all the sisters and brothers we are called to love.

Each time we share in His body and blood it is Easter Sunday. Christ is risen and we share in that life until He comes again to take us home to the Father.

Friday of the Third Week of Easter
Acts 9:1-20, Psalm 117:1-2
John 6:52-59

WHEN WE SHARE IN THE EUCHARIST we take part in the Lord's

Supper. The Eucharist is the sacrifice of the cross and it is the sacrament of his body and blood. It is the meal of the Christian Church. It is the meal to which Jesus invites all to sit down with Him and sup.

The Eucharistic meal is the Meal of the Community. It is the family meal when we all belong not because we are worthy, but because we are loved — passionately and completely.

This means that we who share in the Eucharist are family. We belong to one another as we do to Jesus. The Eucharist makes us one flesh and one body in Jesus Christ. As I approach the Table, I pray for unity and peace with all. I forgive all who have harmed me and I pray for forgiveness of all whom I have hurt. The Eucharist is Genesis all over again. It is creation. It is a new beginning as I am reconciled to all humanity. It is not just the Body of Christ I receive. I receive and become one with all humanity. In Christ, there is no color, nationality, race or religion. We are all God's beloved children called to love one another and to build His new world.

As I leave the Table I am aware of those who are hungry and without a home. The Eucharist burns in the hearts of the followers of Jesus who commit themselves to build a world of justice for all who suffer because of the greed and the hardness of heart of individuals and governments. In each parish where the Eucharist is really celebrated and Jesus is recognized, the works of peace and justice flow. There is no "real presence" of Jesus unless his followers give their lives to achieving peace, justice and dignity for all: the unborn, the poor and homeless child, the prisoner, the abuse victim, the homosexual, and the powerless. The Eucharist is a guarantee that those who are unwanted by society will always have friends to love them and defend them.

Saturday of the Third Week of Easter
Acts 9:31-42, Psalm 116:12-13, 14-15, 16-17
John 6:60-69

ONCE WE GET BEYOND the sterile and lifeless way we often celebrate and receive the Eucharist, we find that we are in very dangerous waters!

What is the Eucharist? Oh, I don't mean what's in the catechism. I mean what is it really? Isn't it ultimately communication, intense communication between Jesus and us? When I receive the Eucharist I am allowing Jesus to love me in a complete and passionate way. He is pouring into my heart His very life and death. He is embracing me, hugging me and kissing me. He is telling me that He loves me so much that He died for me. He is telling me that His love is so intense that it is pledged and given to me in the sign of the new covenant of His very life and death. He is telling me that He will never withdraw His love or His grace; He will be with me and for me forever; He will always love me; He can do nothing else but love me in this way. The Body of Christ. Amen!

And what am I saying as I receive the Eucharist? I too am renewing the Covenant. I am renewing my baptism and the priesthood. I am telling Jesus that I love Him with all my heart and soul and that I want to be His disciple and share that love with all people. I am saying that I embrace Him, as I hug and kiss Him. I am saying that I belong to Him; I repent of my sins and accept His forgiveness. I am telling Him that I will love my neighbor and do His work of peace, justice and love. The Blood of Christ. Amen!

How dangerous is it to come to the Table and eat with Him? When I do so I can never be the same again.

THE FOURTH WEEK OF EASTER

Fourth Sunday of Easter
*John 10:1-10 (Cycle A), John 10:11-18 (Cycle B),
John 10:27-30 (Cycle C)*

THE CHURCH DELIGHTS in hearing the Good Shepherd Gospels. There is something so comforting and appealing in knowing that Jesus is my Good Shepherd. The image that Jesus paints of Himself as Shepherd is that of lover, provider, leader, mother/father and savior.

This Shepherd loves me so much that he willingly lays down His life so that I might live. His death on the cross is the gift of the one who loves me most and desires my personal freedom and wellbeing. This love that I experience is not and can never be the result of my own goodness. It is pure gift waiting to be accepted and lived. As I kneel before the crucifix and look at the face of Jesus, my Good Shepherd, can I ever doubt His love for me again?

The more I believe in and accept Jesus as my shepherd, my lover, my healer, my advocate and my friend, the more I become empowered and inspired to be a good shepherd. In all the relationships in my life there is the opportunity and the call to be shepherd.

It is so true. When I allow Jesus to shepherd me, I instinctively begin to shepherd others and will allow others to shepherd me by their love and friendship. This mutual shepherding is what makes the Church the kingdom of God.

Only those weak enough, poor enough and sinful enough will allow the Son of God to pick them up in His arms and love them. Only those embraced by the Lamb will want to embrace others in His name. Only those who allow themselves to be held will in turn be able to hold others.

Am I weak enough, poor enough, and sinful enough to be held by the Lamb of God?

Monday of the Fourth Week of Easter
Acts 11:1-18, Psalm 42:2-3, 43:3-4
John 10:1-10

THE GOSPEL TODAY continues the Good Shepherd theme. The loving death of the Good Shepherd on the cross is the most powerful image of God's love. In Jesus' death on the cross we witness the "extremes" that the Lord goes to to show us His love.

What is the death of the Lamb of God all about? Did Jesus have to die on the cross? Of course not! The death of the Lamb of God should never be looked at as the price of salvation — what Jesus *had* to do to save us. What kind of a God would demand this kind of payment?

Rather, the death of Jesus should be looked upon as a reckless, unreasonable, extreme and irrational love that God has for you personally. The love of Jesus is so total that He holds back nothing — not even His own life.

Most of the problems in our faith life flow from our inability to believe the Good News of John 3:16, that *"God so loved the world that He gave His only Son."* That love of the Father is celebrated in the most sorrowful/joyful event of history: Jesus lays down His life. He gives it freely for you.

The most powerful and meaningful moment in the life of a Christian is when we kneel before the crucifix and look at the face of Jesus and believe it all for the first time. Because of the great gift of the Holy Spirit we know and say: "Thank you for dying because you loved me so much."

Have you been able to say that yet?

Tuesday of the Fourth Week of Easter
Acts 11:19-26, Psalm 87:1-3, 4-5, 6-7
John 10:22-30

IN TODAY'S GOSPEL Jesus tells us that His sheep hear His voice. They follow Him because He knows them. The image of the shepherd and the flock applies so beautifully to church life and to family life.

What Jesus is really speaking about is His relationship to His people. Jesus leads us and challenges us because He belongs to us and we to Him. The "power" of the Good Shepherd is the total gift of love that He has given to us. We hear His voice. It is the voice of mercy, compassion, healing and trust. It is the voice that soothes us because it is the voice of love. We know and we trust that voice of love because it will only do good for us.

Church life has to be characterized by that same kind of trust and love. Parishes can never really do the wonderful works of Jesus unless they are families. Love and mutual respect have to characterize the life of a parish.

Many parishes put out a good product. They are professional, up-to-date and efficient. The problem is that they are built around efficiency as their basis rather than relationship and love. They become cold places where people do not feel loved, wanted or important.

If a parish is to be real it has to be a place where people experience the love, mercy, tenderness and healing of Jesus. When they do, they will do the mighty and healing works of Jesus and they will touch everyone as Jesus did.

Our homes are no different. We have to work and give our lives as we love one another with all we've got — just like Jesus did. When we are loved like that in our church and in our own home, we have heaven on earth. We experience the Good Shepherd.

What are you doing to make your home and parish the home of Jesus?

Wednesday of the Fourth Week of Easter
Acts 12:24-13: 5, Psalm 67:2-3, 5, 6, 8
John 12:44-50

IN TODAY'S GOSPEL Jesus repeats the theme we find in the first chapter of John. Jesus is the light of the world. St. John told us that the Light shines in the darkness and the darkness has never been able to put it out (John 1).

I remember making my first directed retreat thirty years ago. Early on in the retreat, Sister Thelma Hall, RC gave me the first chapter of John to pray on. I had never really used the Scriptures for prayer before. I remember reading the text of John 1 over a few times and suddenly having a profound sense that Christ was the Light shining in my life.

In spite of the darkness, in spite of my sins and infidelities that Light continues to shine in the darkness. Indeed, the greater the darkness, the brighter the Light of Christ becomes.

That experience of "seeing" the Light of Christ has been repeated many times in my life as I become more aware of His presence.

Christ is brighter and greater than any power of evil. Christ overcomes every evil. Christ is always victorious. Our resurrection faith leads us to seek the Light of Christ and leave the darkness.

When I walk in the Light of Christ there is never anything to hide. His truth can shine on every part of my life. There are no shadows. There is no fear. There is no darkness. I cannot stumble or fall for He leads and lights the way. I truly walk in the Truth.

When I present the newly baptized with their candle I am delighted to say: "Receive the light of Christ. Never fear the darkness, for Jesus, the Light of the world will keep you from all harm. Amen."

Thursday of the Fourth Week of Easter
Acts 13:13-25, Psalm 89:2-3, 21-22, 25, 27
John 13:16-20

TODAY'S GOSPEL takes us back to Holy Thursday and foot washing and the meaning of priesthood — ministerial and baptismal. Each Christian is baptized into the servant ministry of Jesus, especially the priest.

To imitate Jesus is to follow His example of being a servant. It always amazes me how children get the connection of what Jesus is teaching in terms of our service for one another, and adults (myself included) often seem to miss the point.

Children, after the initial giggles, will tell you that Jesus doesn't expect us to literally wash each other's feet (unless of course, we happen to be mommies and daddies or nurses), but that we have to care for one another and help one another, especially the poor and the sick. The kids will tell you that you're supposed to be like Jesus, humble and poor and loving and taking care of everybody. Each Holy Thursday they set us straight!

Why is it that we adults don't always get it? Why do we think that we can devoutly receive Communion and not be involved in areas of justice for all people? How can we receive Him and still close an eye to racism, sexism, homophobia and prejudice of all kinds? Why have we not seen the connection between the Eucharist and the basin? How can the Eucharist not make us uncomfortable to the reality of homelessness, poor children, more welfare cuts and hatred of immigrants?

How is it that our Church considers one's sex and marital status the major determining factors of one's suitability for the priesthood or episcopacy, while it tolerates a clerical state and lifestyle replete with titles and wardrobes that bespeak aloofness, prestige and power? Let's ask the kids. Maybe they can figure it out!

Friday of the Fourth Week of Easter
Acts 13:26-33, Psalm 2:6-7, 8-9, 10-11
John 14:1-6

THIS BEAUTIFUL GOSPEL is proclaimed at many funerals. It is a Gospel of great hope. Jesus is telling us to trust Him. He is calling us from fear to peace. He is assuring us that He is always there for us and that we will not be abandoned.

Lord Jesus, my brother and my friend, I do trust you. I know that you always guide me and protect me. I know that even in the midst of my most terrifying struggles you are there. You get me through them.

Many times, Lord, I don't understand why I or those I love have to go through certain things. Sometimes, they cause me to get angry; often I'm confused. Sometimes I wonder if you're there at all and if you really care what happens. But when I look back I know you were there. I know that you were guiding me and caring for me. I can even see good coming out of things that I thought were hell itself. Paul was right in Romans 8: "All things work together for good for those who love God."

"Dear Jesus, I've seen so many beautiful people go through living deaths and living hells and get through them and be better people than they were before. I've seen people become more loving, more human and more com-

passionate because they went through their personal crucifixions and found you in them.

I've also seen people destroyed in every way through
the burdens of life. Lord, help those sisters and brothers
who are at the edge. Touch them, Lord and let them know
You are there. Please, Lord, be merciful to them."

Saturday of the Fourth Week of Easter
Acts 13:44-52, Psalm 98:1, 2-3, 3-4
John 14:7-14

TODAY JESUS SPEAKS of the intimate union of Himself and the
Father. We often speak as Philip did: "Show us the Father."
Jesus replies to us, "Have I been with you so long and you
still don't know me?"

Is it possible that after a lifetime of Christian living we
don't know who Jesus is? Can it be that we have lived a religion of law, observance and obedience and we don't really
know Jesus?

In the Easter mystery we are called like Thomas to
touch the wounds of Christ and to recognize who He is —
the only Son of the Father and our Beloved Brother.

As we look at Jesus we look at the Father. He is the
living Word made flesh in time in the womb of Mary the
virgin. As we look at Jesus we also see humanity. We see all
the family in the face of Jesus. Jesus is God with us. Jesus is
humanity with us. Jesus is true God of true God. Jesus is the
flesh and blood Son of Mary.

As we acknowledge the identity of Jesus we claim our
own identity. We are the Body of Christ. We are Jesus living
in this time and place. Only when I realize my identity can
I live out my destiny.

I am called to be Christ for you. Jesus assures us that

we will do the works He did and even greater! What plans Jesus has for us. All we have to do is realize who He is and accept who we are and act accordingly. In order to do this He promises and gives us His Holy Spirit. Pentecost is coming soon.

THE FIFTH WEEK OF EASTER

Fifth Sunday of Easter
John 14:1-12 (Cycle A)

IN THIS BEAUTIFUL GOSPEL Jesus speaks of preparing a place for us — a home. Is there any word that touches our hearts like that of "home?" Home is peace. It is love. It is belonging. It is healing and it is forgiveness.

I have always been blessed by having a home to return to. Whether my parents', or my sister and her husband's — home has always been the rudder for me in turbulent times and renewal in peaceful ones.

Home is not a building. It is a relationship of love. Our spiritual life is so enriched when we have a family, when we belong to someone who will always be here for us — in the good times and the bad. Jesus uses the image of the home to exemplify what He meant by heaven and being home with God.

Grace does build on nature. Our best glimpse of heaven and God is living in a healthy and loving home. This is the most important thing we can give to our children. Not only do they need this loving experience to grow psychologically and emotionally, but also a healthy home is the beginning of a healthy and sound spiritual life.

Family life is the first and most authentic eucharist a child ever experiences. The more "eucharistic" home life is, the more a child is able to relate to what happens in church on Sunday.

What a grace and blessing it is when family and friends come together and gather around the table. The stories, the jokes, the sharing of memories and experiences are truly a Liturgy of the Word. High calorie and fat-filled meals with homemade pastas and sauces and desserts, washed down with plenty of good wine are a magnificent Liturgy of the Eucharist. As we recognize Him in the breaking of the Bread of Family and Friendship, we are prepared to recognize Him in the Breaking of the Bread at the Sunday Eucharist.

When I know and experience the sacrament of friendship and family in my home, I am well prepared to embrace the world as my family and celebrate the sacrament of love and unity in all people. It's a very simple step to sit at the Lord's Table after I have sat down at my family's table. In both places we can fully recognize Him in the Breaking of the Bread.

Fifth Sunday of Easter
John 15:1-8 (Cycle B)

PRUNING IS A VERY TRAUMATIC EXPERIENCE for the vine. It's even worse for us! We try to avoid it and get around it, but the Lord at different and critical times in our lives, allows it to happen. If the vine is going to produce the best possible grapes it must not waste its strength on barren or dead branches. It has to give everything it has to the life of the healthy branches.

In our lives we know the same is true. Sometimes the Lord does the pruning directly. Like St. Paul we are knocked off our high horse and have to learn some basic lessons in humility and priorities.

At other times, the Holy Spirit helps us to know that we have to do some personal pruning in our lives. The decision to be a part of a Twelve Step Program is one of those blessed and wonderful moments when a person realizes that they are powerless over alcohol, food, sex, gambling, drugs, etc. (Step 1). This moment of beginning the process of pruning is one of the most painful moments, but also one of the most deeply religious moments in a person's life. It is followed by the realization that a Power greater than ourselves could restore our sanity (Step Two). And then the person makes a decision to turn their will and their life over to the care of God as they understand Him (Step Three).

And so the pruning begins. As the unhealthy and sick branches are pruned from the life of the person, a new life begins to dawn, filled with God's peace and joy.

Probably the greatest movement in All-American spirituality is the 12-Step Program of AA. The principles are solid and Gospel rooted. Is there anything you need to start pruning? Whether you use a 12-Step Program or through private counseling or spiritual direction, the decision to begin is one of the holiest moments in one's life.

Fifth Sunday of Easter
John 13:31-33, 34-35 (Cycle C)

A NEW COMMANDMENT: "Love one another as I have loved you." This sublime call that Jesus gives to His followers is the very heart of the Gospel. We expect Him to tell us to love one another. That philosophy and ethic is found in so many great religions. Jesus adds to it something that makes Christianity unique. We are to love one another *"the way Jesus first loved us."*

How did Jesus love us? He loved us to the end. He poured out His love on the cross by laying down His life for each and every one of us. He held back nothing for Himself. He gave everything. That's how Jesus loved us and that's how Jesus wants us to love one another.

This section from St. John is read at many weddings. Imagine if Pre-Cana and the witness of the Church really

helped the young couple to grasp the power and the meaning of the love that Jesus invites them to be part of, especially in the Sacrament of Marriage!

All of the Family Life ministries of the Church have
one thing in common: to help people grasp the holiness of
their lives by sharing in the love of Jesus.

Couples, parents, single people, celibates — all of us
are called to love with the radical abandonment of Jesus
who doesn't count the cost, but gives everything — His
very self for and to His beloved.

This is the kind of love that will transform us. No
other kind of love will satisfy us. Nothing less will have any
meaning. Are we willing to pray to the Holy Spirit for the
gift of that kind of love?

Monday of the Fifth Week of Easter
Acts 14:5-18, Psalm 115:1-2, 3-4, 15-16
John 14:21-26

TODAY JESUS EQUATES the commandment we have received
from Him with our way of loving Him. Indeed, without
love there is no morality. There is no Church. Love is the
heart of reality.

I remember when I was in the seminary, Fr. Bernard
Haring, CSSR published his great work, *The Law of Christ*.
Fr. Haring did an incredible service with that book to begin
our long pilgrimage to a new morality — one based not on
unending laws and regulations, but one flowing from the
basic law of Christianity — the love of God for us in Christ
Jesus Our Lord.

Fr. Haring challenged us to think beyond legalism,
control and neurotic guilt. He called us to place God and
man above the Law, and not just to seek out the call that

God was giving to us in the context of our traditional morality, but to go far beyond it.

How often law, legalism and religion become ways of avoiding God's will. Jesus found it in His ongoing struggle with the Scribes and Pharisees. That Spirit is alive and well right now and we all are tempted to follow the letter of the law rather than to follow what Jesus is demanding of us through the guidance of the Spirit.

We experience groups in the Church now who are passionate in their adherence to one part of the Gospel of Life but who ignore other parts of that "seamless garment."

Our morality goes beyond law and order. It is based on our relationship and love of God, our neighbor and ourselves. Our moral life grows and matures not by just observing laws but in seeking the will of God for ourselves in all the relationships and responsibilities of our lives. Our conscience is formed not by rote obedience to rules but by the intimate and personal growth of our conscious decisions.

Fr. Haring continues to teach and inspire us. The Lord has called him home, but before his death he published another great book, *Priesthood Imperiled* in which he restates many of the challenging themes of *The Law of Christ*. It is wonderful spiritual reading recommended to all.

Tuesday of the Fifth Week of Easter
Acts 14:19-28, Psalm 145:10-11, 12-13, 21
John 14:27-31

TODAY JESUS TELLS US that He gives us a farewell gift — the gift of Peace — *Shalom*. This gift is so yearned for today. Many people who have everything really have nothing because they don't have peace. What is this elusive gift we all seek?

Peace is interior harmony. It has nothing to do with what is going on outside of me. I can be in the midst of war and I can still be at peace. Peace has more to do with the way I feel about myself than it does with what's going on around me.

Peace is having my life in order. Peace is living in justice. Peace is forgiving and accepting forgiveness. Peace is doing one's best. Peace is relying on the mercy and forgiveness of God. Peace is letting go of the hurts of yesterday and beginning again today.

Peace is living in the joy of personal relationship with Jesus in which I have given my life — including sin and brokenness to the Lord. Peace is trusting in His love and believing that He will never abandon me and that He will be with me through it all.

Peace flows from a life of faith, hope and love. I have known people dying of cancer who were in great peace. They knew who they were and where they were going. I have seen people who have little of the world's wealth and are still very much at peace because they appreciated the wealth of being loved by the Lord and their family.

Jesus loves you so much. He wants you to love his gift of peace. Is there anything in your heart preventing you from enjoying that peace? Isn't it time to get rid of it?

Wednesday of the Fifth Week of Easter

Acts 15:1-6, Psalm 122:1-2, 3-4, 4-5
John 15:1-8

WE REFLECTED ON THIS GOSPEL last Sunday (Cycle B). We prayed about how pruning causes new life and health both to vines and to us.

Today we reflect on the words of Jesus as He tells us

that if we live in Him and if His words are part of us, we may ask for anything and it will be given to us.

What does it mean to live in Him? It means that the mind and heart of Jesus become our mind and heart. How can we achieve such intimacy except by choosing to accept the gift of friendship and love that Jesus is offering to us.

Jesus is offering us his love. He is calling us to a new life, one in which we walk with Him and live with Him in a very personal way. He is calling us to a real prayer life — characterized by our prayer of the heart. We pray in our own words about what's really going on in our life.

Many times people go to prayer with a stack of books and Bibles. That's fine, but what about that deep, silent, intense communication of love between two best friends. Sometimes "prayer" takes us away from *real* prayer because we never talk about what is going on in our hearts.

Imagine a young man head over heels in love with a young woman. If on their dates all they ever did was read from Barrett's *Sonnets from the Portuguese* but never spoke from their hearts, the relationship wouldn't last too long.

Yet, that is what we often do with Jesus. He doesn't desert us but He must get bored. He already knows what's in the Bible. He loved it when St. Theresa spoke to Him in her own words. Right now He'd love to hear what's in your heart. What's holding you back?

Thursday of the Fifth Week of Easter
Acts 15:7-21, Psalm 96:1-2, 2-3, 10
John 15:9-11

WHY DON'T WE BELIEVE we're good enough to be loved by Jesus? Why do we think we are not worthy to love Jesus? We seem to spend so much of our lives living in heresy — denying the core truth of our faith — *"God loved us so much*

He gave His only Son" (John 3:16).

"As the Father has loved me, so I have loved you!" Imagine! Jesus tells us that the eternal, unending love of the Father for Jesus is like the love Jesus has for us.

This is not "here today gone tomorrow" kind of love that we see around us all the time. This is not "I'll love you as long as you are perfect" kind of love that many were brought up with. This is not "I'll love you when you've earned it — after years of penance and suffering" kind of love. This is not "I'll only love you after you make up for all your sins" kind of love. These kinds of love have nothing to do with God or Jesus. They are lies and idols, which must be ground to dust and cast out of our hearts forever.

The love of God for us in Christ Jesus is just too simple and pure for us to believe. Our God is madly in love with us. Our God loves us without condition. He doesn't love us because we're good or because we're bad. He loves us and that's all there is to it.

"Yes, Jesus, you love me. You love me in spite of my infidelities and broken promises. You loved me when I believed in you and when I didn't. You loved me when I was a faithful priest and you loved me when I wasn't. You loved me in my glory and in my misery."

"You love eternally. You'll never stop. When, I look at the crucifix, I know there's nothing more you can do to prove it. Lord, please help my unbelief turn to belief."

Friday of the Fifth Week of Easter
Acts 15:22-31, Psalm 57:8-9, 10-12
John 15:12-17

JESUS TELLS US TODAY that there is no greater love than to lay down one's life for one's friend. This is a very unsettling

Gospel. It's great to talk about Him loving us when it's the-oretical, heady and philosophical. This is not. This is a dead body on a cross, whipped beyond recognition with a crown of thorns on His head. This is the innocent pure One, the Lamb of God who gives His life freely for me because He says I'm His friend.

He won't call me slave or servant. He calls me friend — a friend that has died for me.

Jesus, it would be so much easier to be your servant or slave! I wouldn't have to get involved with all this love and relationship stuff. I could be a good boy and do the right things and go to heaven. The Father's not angry any more because you paid the price He was asking. Some call that being saved.

You won't buy it. You won't let us get away with reli-gion; you want relationship. I try to get by with the salva-tion machine and you let me play Christian and when I think I've won and you've forgotten me, you ruin every-thing and call me "friend." You speak my name and you call me "friend." "I have chosen you to go forth and bear fruit."

Lord, maybe this Pentecost the Holy Spirit will zonk me so hard that I'll stop playing my cute little games (which you see right through) and I'll say, "Yes. Here I am Lord." Maybe.

Saturday of the Fifth Week of Easter
Acts 16:1-10, Psalm 100:1-2, 3, 5
John 15:18-21

JESUS WARNS US about the hatred of the world. Indeed, being a follower of Jesus has become a very dangerous occupa-tion. Archbishop Romero and the other martyrs of El

Salvador alone are a graphic witness to the price that many of His true friends are required to pay.

It is not easy to go against the current. It's not easy to be patronized as a conservative because you're against abortion. It's hard to be thought of as a liberal if you oppose the death penalty. It's tough to let your friends and co-workers know that you don't appreciate racist and anti-Semitic remarks.

It's tough to be looked upon as a dinosaur because you believe that sex belongs in marriage or that condoms aren't the answer to teenage sexual problems. Believing in justice for all people and being against welfare cuts that hurt children and single parents can make you very unpopular. You can be looked upon as anti-American for thinking that we and other nations might find better ways to settle our problems without killing one another. Maybe there really is something wrong with selling weapons and land mines to third and fourth world countries.

Jesus reminds us that if we really are his followers we should expect no better treatment than He got! That's a very hard word to hear. No one wants to be laughed at, ridiculed, hated or even crucified for what they believe.

Only the grace of God and the love and support of the Christian community can get us through it all and give us the courage to pay the price each day for being His friends.

THE SIXTH WEEK OF EASTER

Sixth Sunday of Easter
John 14:15-21 (Cycle A)

IN TODAY'S GOSPEL Jesus continues to pour His heart out to the apostles in the Last Discourse. What tender and loving words they are! How much Jesus loves His dear friends. These words of Jesus are His words to us, His dear friends of today. He loves us just as much as He loved the apostles.

Jesus promises them and us another friend, another advocate, another Paraclete — the Holy Spirit. This new friend, who will come when He leaves, will make Jesus — His work and His love — even more present in our hearts and the world.

Who is the Holy Spirit? Catholic theology has always taught that the Holy Spirit is the love between the Father and the Son and that love is another expression of the loving relationship between the Father and the Son. When Jesus promises the Holy Spirit He is promising to overshadow us with the most powerful and holy force in all creation, God's love.

Jesus promises us that we will not be orphans. We will not be alone. The love of God will fill our lives and our hearts. We will be part of the very love of God and God's love will fill all that we do and all that we are.

This Holy Spirit is the Spirit of love, truth, patience, peace, kindness, mercy, long suffering. The Church since Vatican II has been in the process of rediscovering the Holy Spirit. The flowering of so many modern movements, especially the Charismatic movement, has given new life and power to the community as the Spirit has renewed and transformed individuals and institutions.

As we approach Pentecost it is a wonderful time for us

to pray that Jesus will indeed baptize us in the Holy Spirit so that we may continue the New Pentecost of Pope John XXIII.

Sixth Sunday of Easter
John 15:9-17 (Cycle B)

TODAY'S GOSPEL is so moving. Jesus tells us that He loves us the way the Father loves Him. Think of how much you are loved! Think of what you mean to Jesus! His love can never be earned or deserved. It is a pure gift.

But a gift presents choices. I can accept the gift or refuse it. Our unending challenge and call is to accept the love that Jesus wished to give to us. Our conversion is to remove the barriers that still stand in the way of embracing the God of love who wants so much to be our friend and who is constantly offering this precious gift of His love. We pray that the Holy Spirit will move us to accept that which Jesus is always offering.

Jesus wants His love to bring us His joy. His joy can never be taken from us. His joy is the fruit of peace that fills our hearts with His presence. When we allow other things to fill our hearts we run the risk of losing His joy.

Jesus tells us that He gives us a new commandment: to love one another as He loved us. What a challenge that is! What a call for husband and wife, parents and children, sisters and brothers and friends to love one another the way Jesus loved us first! I frequently use this scripture at a wedding ceremony. Jesus speaks this word to the young couple. *"Love one another as I have loved you"* (John 15). I always point to the crucifix and remind the couple that this is how Jesus loved them. I ask them if they are willing to love each other in that way.

Imagine the world when we all make the decision to

love the way Jesus loved us first. Imagine what would happen as we lovingly and willingly lay down our lives in love for one another! The Kingdom of God would truly be among us.

Sixth Sunday of Easter
John 14:23-29 (Cycle C)

JESUS PROMISES the Holy Spirit to us. Jesus assures us that the Holy Spirit will instruct us in everything and remind us of everything that He taught us. The Holy Spirit has quite a job description and has never let us down.

As the time for Jesus to leave us approaches, He promises us that it is good for us that He leaves. He tells us not to be afraid or distressed, because the coming of the Holy Spirit will make the presence of Jesus more powerful than when He was physically present.

As sad as it is to have Him leave us, it is true: Jesus is more present on this earth today than when He walked the roads of Galilee. The Holy Spirit makes Him present in the hearts and lives of all His disciples who walk their own roads today and who do even greater things than Jesus was able to do when He was physically present.

The Holy Spirit continues to create the Church. It is Genesis and it is Pentecost every time we pray "Come Holy Spirit!" Jesus continues to live in us through the indwelling of the Spirit and we continue to do His powerful and wonderful works.

Let us pray now that our hearts be truly open this Pentecost to make room for the coming of the Holy Spirit. Let us pray that the Spirit overpowers us and that we allow God to live in us and rule our lives with His peace and His joy. Amen!

Monday of the Sixth Week of Easter
Acts 16:11-15, Psalm 149:1-2, 3-4, 5-6, 9
John 15:26-16:4

IN TODAY'S SCRIPTURE Jesus talks to us about "troubles" and persecution. It is a sobering pause from the positive and reassuring messages of these Easter Days. It is however, very realistic and very necessary for us to hear.

Jesus never promised us a garden of roses. He never promised us a life without sickness, unemployment, radiation treatments, chemotherapy, depression, suicidal teenagers, divorce, separations, falling out of love, temptation, persecution and even death. The cross is part and parcel of all of our lives.

While we don't go out looking for trouble, we know that the shadow of the cross falls upon all of us and those whom we love.

What Jesus did promise us is that he would be with us in the dark moments and that His grace would sustain us and get us through whatever would come into our lives. He will sustain us and He will be there for us.

The mystery of Jesus is His death and resurrection. We know that there would have been no Resurrection without Jesus first lovingly embracing the cross. As we live the Paschal Mystery we also have to pass through the mystery of the cross if we are to be able to celebrate the glory and joy of the Resurrection. It is the cross, which purifies us and makes us capable of understanding and living the new life which Jesus wishes us to possess.

Jesus is not our Savior to prevent us from embracing the pain of life, but rather our brother to be there for us to help us in living and passing through to the resurrection.

Tuesday of the Sixth Week of Easter

Acts 16:22-34, Psalm 138:1-2, 2-3, 7-8
John 16:5-11

JESUS CONTINUES THE THEME of yesterday in today's Gospel. He speaks to us about how it will be better for us if He leaves us and sends us the new advocate — the Holy Spirit. This is a very bitter pill for the apostles to swallow. What could possibly be better than having the Jesus they love so much physically present to them? What could be better than speaking to Jesus, eating with Him and listening to Him?

Yet, it is better that He left. His Spirit has transformed the whole world. Look at what the Church has done in the absence of Jesus! The Gospel is preached to all people; the poor are taken care of; the brokenhearted are comforted — all by the Body of Christ — His Church. On Pentecost, as the Church was born, a whole new reality of the presence and ministry of Jesus began.

What seemed to be the end was really a new beginning. We would be empowered by the Holy Spirit to do greater and more wonderful things than Jesus did as He walked this earth. Think of all His disciples who walk the earth today in His footsteps and continue His glorious and beautiful works.

There is a lesson here for us: what seems to be the end may really be the beginning; what seems to be defeat may actually be victory and what appears to be death may actually be a new birth.

Doesn't it all depend on how willing we are to place our life and its problems in the hands of Jesus with perfect trust and confidence? How many new beginnings is Jesus accomplishing in your life right now?

Wednesday of the Sixth Week of Easter
Acts 17:15, 22-18:1, Psalm 148:1-2, 11-12, 12-14
John 16:12-15

IN TODAY'S GOSPEL Jesus tells us that there are many things He must tell us but we cannot hear them now. The Holy Spirit will teach us about them.

In some ways this can seem like a "put down." Why can't I hear it now? Am I not mature enough? The answer is: No! Our lives with Jesus are a journey and a process. We learn about Jesus and ourselves and the meaning of our lives gradually. The Holy Spirit does not teach us everything all at once but gives us the tools to uncover and discover all that Jesus wants us to know. This process takes a lifetime. It cannot be rushed. We cannot skip steps and jump ahead. We learn from day to day — minute to minute.

This learning process of what Jesus wants to teach us does not happen automatically. It only happens when one is open to the movement of the Spirit in one's prayer life and in all the events of one's life. There has to be a reflective part of our lives in which there is room and quiet for the Holy Spirit to speak and love us.

When our lives are filled with constant and strident noise, and useless and exhausting activity, we set obstacles to the Spirit to teach and lead us.

As we approach this Pentecost it is a good time to re-evaluate our personal readiness and willingness to allow the Spirit to move our hearts and to teach us the meaning of life.

As we grow in the life of the Spirit we become more able "to hear" all that Jesus is telling us about His Father and about the love the Father has for us. The telling is not a crash course. It is gentle, gradual and daily. There is no rushing it. It presumes and demands a life-long walk with the Spirit. The final chapter of what the Spirit has to teach us will be written when the Lord welcomes us home and calls us by name. In the meantime, it is a wonderful adventure and journey. Don't deprive yourself of walking every step of it.

Ascension Thursday
Acts 1:1-11, Psalm 96:1-2, 2-3, 10, Ephesians 1:17-23
Matthew 28:16-20 *(Cycle A),* **Mark 16:15-20** *(Cycle B),*
Luke 24:46-53 *(Cycle C)*

TODAY'S FIRST READING from Acts thrills me, not just for its beauty and grandeur but because it was the first Scripture reading I ever heard in English (since the change to the vernacular). I was the lector! I will always look back with fondness to that day at the Lake Ronkonkoma Cenacle in 1957 when the Liturgy came alive for me for the first time. God bless the Cenacle for making many things come alive for me!

In that reading, the angels ask a very important question: "Men and women of Galilee, why do you stand here looking up to heaven? This Jesus will return." Early on in the life of the Church we are faced with the conflict of the "looking up to heaven" spirituality vs. the "let's get to work" spirituality. I don't think we will ever reconcile it completely. The Martha/Mary syndrome is always at work in the Church and in our own hearts. We know that we need the "heavenly" respites of prayer and meditation and we also know that we are called to work very hard to build the Kingdom of God. Both must be present in our lives — prayer and work. The more we pray; the more work we see that must be done. The more work we do; the more we need to pray.

Rather than looking at these two parts of our lives as enemies, perhaps we should see them as complementing one another. One really flows from the other and one completes the other. Prayer without work is narcissism. Work without prayer becomes feverish activity that has no grounding.

As we grow in the Spirit, we become more and more apt at integration. Integration is at the heart of maturity. The Spirit tells us how much and what we should do and also how much and when we must pray. Come, Holy Spirit!

Friday of the Sixth Week of Easter
Acts 18:9-18, Psalm 47:2-3, 4-5, 6-7
John 16:20-23

IN TODAY'S GOSPEL Jesus speaks of the weeping and mourning that the disciples will endure, but promises us that the tears will be turned to joy.

Jesus then gives the example of the woman in labor about to give birth to a child and how all that pain and fear is completely turned into joy when she beholds the child she brought into the world.

Isn't the life of the Christian very similar? Don't we often go through fears and pain and other kinds of labor? Yet, when we are faithful and when we don't let go of Jesus, He turns what was pain and even at times hell, into peace and joy. At the heart of that peace and joy is the knowledge that He has not let go of us and He has taken care of us. Eventually, hopefully, we are even able to say "thank you" for what the Lord allowed us to endure.

In this time of preparation for Pentecost, it is a very helpful thing to go back over the terrible moments of labor and giving birth in our lives, taking the time to see how the

Lord brought us through. Sometimes it's good to remember them just to see how Jesus has been Savior to us. We know that we could never have gotten through them without Him. Think of them and thank Him.

Hopefully, these new births made us softer and kinder people, more gentle and more compassionate. As a result of the new births, Jesus promised us His joy and His peace. Is that part of who you are now? Have you grown into that man or woman who is truly human and thus truly spiritual? Not yet? That's why the Holy Spirit is coming to you again.

Saturday of the Sixth Week of Easter
Feast of Our Lady of the Cenacle
Acts 18:23-28, Psalm 47:2-3, 8-9, 10
John 16:23-28

TODAY'S FEAST of Our Lady of the Cenacle is special and unique to the Sisters of the Cenacle and all those generations of children and friends who found a special love of the Lord and His mother through their witness and their teaching.

Acts 1:14 is the heart of this feast — the disciples, women and men at prayer with Mary in the Upper Room in the Cenacle — waiting for the coming of the Holy Spirit.

This prayer with Mary is the heart of the infant Church and the heart of the Church today. Mary is always calling her children to prayer. This Marian prayer is not meant to be an escape from the world, but rather an openness to the presence and the prompting of the Holy Spirit — the opportunity for Mary to say her "yes" and to live it with fidelity.

The Spirit leads Mary to her vow of virginity — to be

totally available to the Lord. Her call to marriage and motherhood was to devote her life to Joseph and Jesus. Mary reminds each Christian that we all have to be "virgins" and we all have to be "married." No matter what our vocation — single, celibate or married — there has to be part of us that belongs only to God. There also has to be part of us committed to people. We have to belong to "someone" or our virginity decays into narcissistic self-centeredness. At the same time we have to belong to "no one" if there is going to be the possibility of sharing our true self with anyone.

Mary is the first and true Charismatic in the Church. She is the model of the believer open to the movement of the Spirit. She is the true disciple who provides space in her heart to listen and to be led by the Holy Spirit. We have no greater Pentecost model than Our Lady of the Cenacle.

THE SEVENTH WEEK OF EASTER

Seventh Sunday of Easter
John 17:1-11 (Cycle A), *John 17:11-19 (Cycle B)*,
John 17:20-26 (Cycle C)

AS THE CHURCH IS YEARNING for the coming of the Holy Spirit, Jesus speaks to His disciples about unity, keeping us from evil and living in His truth — no small matters! As Jesus pours out His heart in John 17, it is as if He were speaking to us today.

The Church is in need of unity. Unity comes from the Holy Spirit but it is only possible to exist in the hearts of believing and loving Christians. Unity is not agreeing with the politics or theology of another, unity is loving another and respecting the right of another to speak their mind and have their opinions. If we truly believe that the Spirit will guide the Church and take care of it, we must humbly listen to other opinions, and allow the Spirit to lead me as I constantly re-evaluate and reflect on what I believe is the truth. Instead of hating opposition, the Christian should rejoice in it!

We really need to be people *of* the Truth, not just doctrinal or magisterial Catholics. The Spirit calls us to personal truth and integrity. We should be transparent. The light of Jesus should shine through us. There should never be duplicity, untruth or manipulation in us. We should say "yes" when we mean "yes' and "no" when we mean "no" — all else, Jesus tells us, comes from the Evil One. Say what you mean and mean what you say.

Jesus prays that we will be preserved from evil. We must also preserve one another. We need one another to affirm us in our values and to encourage us to continue to be faithful to the Lord.

We also need to encourage and protect our children. God only knows what they face today on the school bus or at school. Their homes have to be places of love and safety where they will be loved and guided so that they will not be led astray by outside influences. Our children need us to love them so much that they know we're "nuts" about them and that we would be willing to die for them. That's what every child deserves. That's what Pentecost will help to bring about in our lives.

Monday of the Seventh Week of Easter
Acts 19:1-8, Psalm 68:2-3, 4-5, 6-7
John 16:29-33

IN TODAY'S GOSPEL Jesus speaks to the apostles about faith. They assure Him that they believe and He responds by asking: Do you really believe?

They have no clue of what will be expected of them in their act of faith. They don't see the next day's horror. They know nothing of the cross, nothing of the fear that will grip them and the despair that will scatter them. Like us, they have no idea of what faith will demand.

Jesus tells them that they will be scattered and that they will lose everything, but yet they will not, because the Holy Spirit will gather them together again and they will find peace.

This peace does not come for them or us by being perfect. Their peace didn't come because they were faithful. They did not stand at the foot of Jesus' cross. They did not profess Him as their Lord. They did not choose to die with Him.

Their peace came through forgiveness. Their peace came to them as ours does, because they had a God whose love for them was not based on perfection or fidelity, but on His unchanging love for each of us. Forgiveness is the nature of our passionate God whose mother/father love for us has nothing to do with what we do or don't do. We experience forgiveness when we decide to accept it. It is always being offered to us. Our conversion is not in deserving or being worthy of God's love, but in simply accepting it. Our God is always offering the gift. God is always loving us. Our challenge is to take from the hands of God what is constantly being offered.

The Easter sacrament is the celebration of the unending gift of love or forgiveness that is always there for us. Each Easter, each day, Peter, James, Judas, you and I have the chance to begin again. Alleluia!

Tuesday of the Seventh Week of Easter
Acts 20:17-27, Psalm 68:10-11, 20-21
John 17:1-11

TODAY JESUS TELLS US eternal life consists in knowing the only true God and He Whom He sent, Jesus Christ. The Church is imploring Jesus at this time to send the Holy Spirit so that we may come to that knowledge.

Part of the agenda of the Holy Spirit is to lead us away from knowledge of false gods to the knowledge of and the love of the one true God. That seems like an extreme statement but it really isn't. Idolatry is alive and well in many of our lives. We do not subscribe to the crude type of idolatry of the Book of Exodus when the Hebrews adored the golden calf. Our brand is much more sophisticated, but just as real.

Church people delight in excoriating the evils of materialism, money, sex, comfort and worldliness of all types.

The presumption is that people who are part of the Church are far removed from such base and human pursuits. In reality, we have a set of idols that may be less obvious, but they prevent us just as effectively from knowing and loving the one true God.

Power is an old and tested idol of Church people. Very often we are much more comfortable with laws and rules and regulations that can control people, rather than seeking what they need.

Manipulation is a trusted bedfellow of power — use and abuse people for one's own needs and objectives, rather than responding to the pleas and requests of people in their real struggles. Manipulation always runs along with deception and dishonesty.

Our work that seems to be so virtuous can become an end in itself. When we work too much and don't foster our relationships with family and friends, that activity has become a sort of idol.

When "churchfolk" become overly concerned with all its human and worldly parts rather than with the will of Him who is the head of the Church, it too becomes an idol. Instead of *serving* Him with programs and stewardship, they become the end in themselves.

Is there anything in your life that has taken the place of Jesus? That is your idol and that is what you must ask the Spirit to remove so that you come to a new knowledge and love of God and His Son Jesus.

Wednesday of the Seventh Week of Easter
Acts 20:28-38, Psalm 68:29-30, 33-35, 35-36
John 17:11-19

IN TODAY'S GOSPEL Jesus prays for the disciples and He

prays for us. Jesus offers a beautiful and touching prayer to the Father asking Him to protect us from the evil that surrounds us and from the world that is not yet part of His Kingdom.

The prayer that Jesus offered to the Father is still offered for all who try to follow Jesus. It is not easy to be a Christian and the Church has to be part of the answer of the prayer of Jesus.

The community of the Church is the place where Jesus is able to protect His people. When we come to Mass on Sunday it is not just to worship the Lord, it is also to be with people with values and dreams similar to our own. There is such a healing and confirming power to be with individuals and families who are trying to live the Gospel values. It's so reassuring to know that there are other "crazies" just like ourselves who believe in this Jesus' stuff and who are trying to live it.

When we share in fellowship after Mass, this healing and confirming continues. The Body of Christ grows in holiness and unity and we fulfill the prayer of Jesus to the Father as we protect and take care of one another. By so doing we transform the world into a place of healing, love and peace. Our world becomes the Kingdom and we are able to enter the other and bring love and peace to it. Once we have experienced the love of the family of God, we have something to bring to that world that doesn't yet know His love.

We are the answer to the prayer of Jesus. We bring His love to the world by establishing His Kingdom right here and now in our own home and parish. As we take care of, love and affirm one another, Jesus can say "thank you" to the Father because His prayer has been answered.

Thursday of the Seventh Week of Easter
Acts 22:30; 23:6-11, Psalm 16:1-2, 5, 7-8, 9-10, 11
John 17:20-26

TODAY IN THE GOSPEL Jesus again tells us that He prays for us — all those who hear His word and believe through the testimony of His disciples. This "testimony and believing" cycle will never end until Jesus returns. We will always have the thrill and the challenge of telling the Good News and the tradition to another generation. The cycle goes on and on, one family passing it on to another — one generation passing it on to another.

The incredible thing is that today's man and woman of faith is capable of knowing and loving Jesus more deeply and more intimately than did the disciples themselves! Time and geography do not determine faith, only love and openness to the Lord can do that. The faith of the saints of today is often stronger than that of those who believed because they saw and heard Jesus with their own eyes and ears!

Our personal loving relationship has no limits placed on it. We are able to know, love and follow Him more faithfully than the eyewitnesses did. Look all around you. See what faith and love in Jesus can do for people. I see people — holy people — the saints — each and every day. Many have difficult lives, but they never let go of Jesus. They have not seen the historical Jesus with their own eyes but you'd never know that by observing their lives.

Each day I see single parents being mother and father to their children and doing beautiful jobs. Jesus is always with them. I see holy people going through the pain of a divorce, but never letting go of Jesus. I see beautiful people going for chemotherapy and radiation treatments holding on to Jesus and never letting go of Him. Everywhere we look in the Church we can see faithful followers of Jesus living lives of heroic sanctity. Even though they haven't seen Him, they believe Him and they follow Him.

Friday of the Seventh Week of Easter
Acts 25:13-21, Psalm 103:1-2; 11-12, 19-20
John 21:15-19

TODAY WE MOVE to chapter 21 of John's Gospel to the past resurrection scene of Peter's profession of faith and contrition. We are actually privileged to eavesdrop on the first confession.

Remember on Holy Thursday that Peter denies Jesus three times. He curses and swears three times that he does not know Jesus; he does not know who He is. Today, Jesus invites Peter to atone for the triple denial by making a triple profession of faith and sorrow for his denial.

"Peter, son of John, do you love me?" Jesus asks. Simon Peter responds: *"Yes, Lord, you know I love you."* Jesus replies: *"Feed my sheep."* At the third questioning Peter is sad. That sadness stems from the fact that Peter feels that Jesus cannot trust him because of the triple denial. Perhaps there is another explanation.

Perhaps Jesus wants the person who will hold such great authority and power to know what personal sin is and to know what it means to need forgiveness. Maybe Jesus was thinking of the times when Peter would have to pass judgment on other people and how hard and intolerant Peter could be to other people's weaknesses and sins. Maybe Jesus thought it would be good for Peter and for the Church to have him publicly confess and be in the shoes of the person coming with hat in hand for forgiveness and mercy.

Maybe Jesus was thinking of how easy it becomes for the servants of Jesus — popes, mothers, fathers, clergy — to become self-righteous, judgmental, "holier than thou" to our sisters and brothers. Maybe Jesus wanted you and me to read this Gospel so that we would never forget our own sinfulness and how we are called to give to one another the gift that Jesus gave to Peter and to us — forgiveness. He said: "Feed my sheep," not, "condemn my sheep."

Saturday of the Seventh Week of Easter
Acts 28:16-20, 30-31, Psalm 11:4, 5, 7
John 21:20-25

TODAY IS THE FINAL DAY of the Easter Season. We celebrate its completion today at the Pentecost Vigil and tomorrow on Pentecost Day. It has been a glorious celebration, a great party for fifty days.

Today's Gospel brings to light something that is only hinted at in the Gospels in other places: sibling rivalry. Peter looking at John says to Jesus: "But Lord what about him?" The context of the passage indicates that Peter is jealous of the special love that Jesus has for John. John was obviously the fair-haired boy — Jesus' favorite.

Can you see yourself in Peter? Can you identify with what is in his heart? It was all well and good that Jesus made Peter the pope, but he wanted more than that. He wanted to be the favorite. He wanted to be number one!

How human the first pope is! How like us. All the love and affection that Jesus had for Peter was not enough because he didn't have it all. How many times we fail to live up to our potential or accomplish wonderful things because we want more and we won't be satisfied with what we've got? How many friendships sour? How many relationships die because we need and demand more that what another is able to give?

And yet, how understandable. Why wasn't Jesus able to love Peter the way He loved John? A very important question! Jesus was also human and He (just like us) loved different people in different ways. Maybe we have a special friend in Peter who will pray for us when we feel the pain of jealousy and maybe Jesus will help us in those moments for certainly there were people who hurt Jesus the way He hurt Peter. It is beautiful to be human, but it is also painful.

The Great Vigil of Pentecost
Genesis 11:1-9, Exodus 19:3-8, 16-20, Ezekiel 37:1-14, Joel 3:1-5, Romans 8:22-27
John 7:37-39

IN MANY PARISHES throughout the world, the community is beginning to take the advice of the ordo and celebrate extended Pentecost Vigils along the same lines as the Easter Vigil. While the emphasis at the Easter vigil is baptism, the emphasis at the Pentecost Vigil is prayer for the Coming of the Holy Spirit and baptism in the Holy Spirit.

We begin outside around the Pentecost fire. Each person is given a piece of wood and asked to write on it the gift of the Holy Spirit that they are praying for. Each person places that piece of wood and petition into the great fire as a fervent prayer begging for the coming of the Spirit.

We then process into Church for an extended Liturgy of the Word. People are encouraged to share a Scripture that touched them in a special way. As part of the homily, people who were baptized at the Easter Vigil give a testimony of their faith journey and conversion. It is always a very moving moment in the life of the parish.

The Liturgy of the Word and the faith sharing leads us to the moment of praying for the release of the Spirit or baptism in the Holy Spirit for all present. We pray that the Spirit will renew in each of us the grace and power of our baptism, confirmation, Holy Communion, marriage, religious profession, ordination, commitments of friendship and service to the community. We pray for the Holy Spirit to renew us in the power and the fervor of the love of God.

The Eucharist then celebrates all that we are as the Body of Christ and renews us in the Spirit of Jesus to be the Body of Christ in this world. After the Mass we continue the celebration as we go "From Holy Hour to Happy Hour!"

Pentecost Sunday
Acts 2:1-11, Psalm 104:1, 24, 29-30, 31, 34,
1 Corinthians 12:3-7, 12-13
John 20:19-23

TODAY THE CHURCH CELEBRATES a glorious birthday party — wearing red garments and singing the great Alleluias! The Church is born as Jesus breathes upon it His Holy Spirit.

One cannot celebrate Pentecost without remembering the great pope of Pentecost, John XXIII, who prayed for a New Pentecost at the beginning of Vatican Council II. The Church continues to pray for the New Pentecost.

Pentecost means life. It means dynamism; it means excitement. Unfortunately, many of those faces who come to Church do not reflect life-giving qualities to the world. We are often perceived as God's frozen people rather than God's holy people.

As the Spirit pours out upon us the love and excitement of the Living God, we must have hearts ready to embrace that new life. It is not enough just to be baptized, confirmed, ordained or married. Each person must personally and constantly implore the Spirit to ignite into flame the sparks and power that these sacraments give to us. Sometimes the embers almost go out and they have to be rekindled. Our life-long process of conversion is nothing more than allowing the Holy Spirit to overpower us and renew the love in our hearts.

All the modern movements of the Spirit in the Church — Marriage Encounter, Home Retreats, Cursillo, Baptism in the Holy Spirit — are meant to set the scene for us to be ready for the coming of the Holy Spirit.

A Life in the Spirit Seminar (see page 89) can be a life-changing event for you as you prepare by penance, prayer and sharing to ask Jesus to give you the Spirit to rekindle the sparks of love in your heart. Once it has happened to you, you can never be the same again.

Come Holy Spirit, fill the hearts of your faithful. Kindle in them the fire of your love and send your Spirit and they shall be created and renew the face of the earth. Amen. Alleluia!

A NEW PENTECOST

(This chapter was written in collaboration with Rev. Claude D'Souza, Edna Clavin, John and Mary Ellen Graham, Dr. Achilles and Leonora Rances and all members of the St. Brigid's Parish Community in Westbury, New York.)

AT THE BEGINNING OF VATICAN II in 1962 Pope John XXIII prayed for a new Pentecost. Little did the world realize then how powerfully the good pope's prayer would be answered. Not only did the Spirit give life and substance to the discussions and eventual documents of the Council, but She also began to bring life and power to communities and individual Christians who opened their hearts and prayed for the coming of the Holy Spirit to release their gifts.

The days since Vatican II saw an explosion of the presence of the Spirit in the Catholic Church that resembled the life of the early Church. Baptism in the Spirit, tongues, prophecy and healing became everyday experiences in the life of the Church. What was once read about with wonder and nostalgia in the Scriptures became the usual stuff of Charismatic prayer groups in the Church. As usually happens when the Church experiences a new movement of grace in a particular community, it soon made its effects felt in the general prayer life and worship of the Church. Liturgies became more lively and open to the prompting of the Spirit both on the part of the clergy and the people.

We truly have been living in a new Pentecost. The prayer of good Pope John was heard and the Church has since been developing and living out a new theology of the Holy Spirit.

Who is the Holy Spirit?

BEFORE WE BEGIN TO CONSIDER the movement of the Spirit in the post Vatican II Church, there is a more basic question to ask: "Who is the Holy Spirit?"

Our catechism taught us as children that the Holy Spirit is God, the third person of the Blessed Trinity. We pray in our Creed each Sunday that the Holy Spirit proceeds from the Father and the Son. Interestingly, the Eastern and Western Church broke apart over that doctrine in 1066 AD. The Eastern Church believed that the Holy Spirit, like the Son, proceeded only from the Son. The "filioque" controversy is only now beginning to be healed between the two churches.

Scripture and tradition refer to the Holy Spirit by many names and titles: Breath, Advocate, Paraclete, Counselor, Spirit of Truth. All of them point to one thing — the Holy Spirit is the life, power and love of God poured out upon the world. It is the Holy Spirit who overshadows the Blessed Virgin Mary at the Annunciation. It is the Holy Spirit who acts powerfully to bring the grace of God to us in the sacraments, especially baptism, confirmation and holy orders. It is the Holy Spirit who inspires the Scriptures and brings the presence of Jesus to the Eucharist.

The Holy Spirit gives life, joy and power to the Church. In the Spirit is the presence and the loving joy of God's passionate love of the Church for all She is and does.

When good Pope John prayed for the New Pentecost he was implying that while the Spirit was present in the Church, the effects of the Spirit's presence were not felt or experienced as they should be. The Spirit was contained and inhibited by a Church that seemed to be afraid of change. It was a Church frozen in time by mistrust and fear of new beginnings. The pope prayed for a spiritual revolution which would change the Church and the entire world forever. The Church began the process of becoming the sacrament of God's life rather than a museum safeguarding old treasures.

The Spirit Was Waiting

THE PHENOMENA THAT WAS EXPERIENCED in the Catholic Church beginning in the sixties had been part and parcel of many of the non-mainstream evangelical churches for almost a century. Indeed many of these communities looked upon the Catholic Church as existing in a very superficial way filled with superstition rather than God's life. Unfortunately, many still do.

A New Day in the Catholic Church

IN 1967, from February seventeenth to the nineteenth, a group of faculty and students from Duquesne University went on retreat. They made this retreat to beg for the outpouring of the gifts of the Holy Spirit they had read about in Acts. They were people of great faith and devotion, who saw the Spirit moving in other Churches. They knew that something was missing in their faith, prayer and relationships.

It was here that what we call the Catholic Pentecostal Movement began. This little community experienced the signs and wonders of apostolic times. Many experienced the baptism of the Holy Spirit and were given many of the gifts of the Holy Spirit.

This was a true turning point in the history of the Catholic Church not only in the United States but also in the whole world. A new day was beginning and a new spirituality was taking form as the experience of this group began to spread like wildfire all over the United States and eventually the entire world. A new understanding of the role of the Holy Spirit in the Church's life was taking root. The reliance upon the gifts of the Spirit became a new and cherished part of Catholic life and practice. It is no exaggeration to say that this new Pentecostal or charismatic movement began to create a new Church, much more Scripture-based and dependent upon the inspiration and movement of the Holy Spirit rather than the rigidity and safety of traditional formulas.

As people became more open to and aware of the role of the Spirit in their lives, beautiful things happened in the everyday life of normal Catholic Christians. There was a new understanding of the Spirit and openness to what the Spirit was saying in our daily prayer. The Holy Spirit was no longer the sole domain of the hierarchy. Ordinary Christians believed and lived as if the Spirit was present and active in their normal everyday lives.

The Holy Spirit used to be the one to whom we prayed before exams for wisdom and knowledge. We now recognize the Spirit as the one who dwells within us, leading us to Jesus and the Father. This recognition greatly influences our prayer, reading of Scriptures, Eucharist and service to the community.

The Spread of Prayer Groups

As PRAYER GROUPS began to spread like wildfire, a pattern of life began to emerge. The key experience in the Charismatic movement was baptism of the Holy Spirit. The teaching of the Church is that at baptism the Holy Spirit overshadows us and fills us with gifts. These gifts are confirmed, or strengthened, in the sacrament of confirmation. Yet, in the lives of most of us, these gifts remain inactive or under-developed.

Baptism in the Holy Spirit adds nothing to sacramental baptism and confirmation. What it does do is lead the believer to beg for the coming of the Holy Spirit so that what is already there might come to life and power.

A person is led to baptism in the Holy Spirit by a course called *Life in the Spirit Seminar.* The seminar lasts about six weeks, during which the candidate participates in a basic course in Christian living: repentance, the sacrament of Reconciliation, daily Scripture meditation and recitation of prayer for the coming of the Holy Spirit.

Toward the end of the seminar, the team and gathered community lay hands on the candidate and pray that the Holy Spirit will fire up the embers of faith, hope and love in the candidate's heart and that he/she will be born again and become a new creation.

Signs and Wonder

AS THE COMMUNITY PRAYS over the candidate for the stirring of the Gifts of the Spirit, it is the same Spirit that transformed the holy women and men in the Upper Room on Pentecost. The same gifts are described in St. Paul's first Letter to the Corinthians, chapters 12 and 13 and in Galatians 5.

The community prays for the gift of tongues. Tongues can be prayer tongues (the most frequent). There is no need to interpret prayer in tongues. It is a personal gift used to praise and glorify the Lord in community prayer settings, and also in private prayer. The late Cardinal Suenens, considered by many to be the father of the modern charismatic movement, felt that the elaborate and extended melodies sung over a single letter or phrase in Gregorian chant were also a type of this personal gift of tongues.

Interpretation is always associated with what is called prophetic tongues. Prophetic tongues are meant to be interpreted and are closely associated with the gift of prophecy. Prophetic tongues is usually interpreted to present a message of exhortation (frequent), proclamation (occasionally), admonition (rare) and consolation (most frequent).

This gift requires great discernment on the part of the prayer group leadership in determining its validity — i.e., whether it is inspired by the Holy Spirit or the spirit of the interpreter. As with the gift of prophecy, the interpretative prophetic message calls upon the listeners to respond or to act upon the message, depending upon its content.

Prophecy is another gift which is prayed for. It is the ability to allow the Spirit to speak through the person with a message to the whole Church. The gift of healing is also begged for. Ordinary people can become the instruments of God's healing for another in body, mind and spirit.

These and other manifestations of the Spirit have become a part of the ordinary life of Charismatic prayer groups and of the entire Church.

The Giver of Gifts

THROUGH BAPTISM, confirmation, orders and the baptism in the Holy Spirit, the Church prays for the Holy Spirit to pour upon the person(s) all of her gifts and blessings — wisdom, understanding, counsel, knowledge, fortitude, piety, fear of the Lord, charity, joy, peace, patience, kindness, goodness, fidelity, gentleness and self-control.

St. Paul in the first Letter to the Corinthians, Chapter 13, writes his magnificent hymn to honor the greatest of all the Spirit's gifts — the gift of love. None of the other gifts mean anything without love. When we are filled with the gift of love we may or may not have any of the other gifts. It doesn't matter; we don't need anything but love. *"In the end there remaineth these three: faith, hope and love, but the greatest of these is love"* (1 Cor. 13).

The Spirit Is Not Contained

LITERALLY, HUNDREDS OF THOUSANDS of Catholics (soon followed by many in mainline Protestant churches) were baptized in the Holy Spirit and continue to be so. The Holy Spirit is not limited to the Charismatic movement and comes in various ways to people. What seems to be necessary is that people desire the Spirit in a fuller way.

The Holy Spirit has provided other beautiful vehicles for the touch of the Holy Spirit. The Marriage Encounter, Renew 2000, Home Retreats, Ignatian Spiritual Exercises, Better World Movement are just some of the few devices the Spirit has used to ready the soul of a believer for the lighting of the fire.

The graces and fruits of the Charismatic movement have touched the whole Church. There is now a greater awareness and openness of the role of the Holy Spirit. Healing ministry and apostolates of service have become integral parts of parish life in many places. There is an eagerness to study the Scriptures. Preaching is much more spirit filled in the Church but has a long way to go.

More than ever before, Catholics now seem to truly

believe the old teaching that they are the temples of the Holy Spirit. They are comfortable with the truth that the Spirit dwells within them. They are ready and more willing to trust themselves in their conscience decisions.

Many Catholics who are not active in the Charismatic movement are being profoundly influenced by the Renewal in their personal and parish spiritual life. Our understanding of the Church as the People of God, along with Vatican II's restoration of the Scriptures and the liturgy to the people are truly profound and charismatic experiences of the Holy Spirit Church.

Parish Prayer Groups

IF YOU WOULD LIKE TO DEEPEN your own life in the Holy Spirit and possibly be baptized in the Holy Spirit I suggest that you join your local parish's Prayer Group. They gather weekly in the spirit of Jesus to give praise and honor to the Father in song and community prayer. They intercede for the needs of those present and the whole world. They minister to those who request the laying on of hands and healing. They share the Holy Scriptures and are open to the presence of the gifts of the Holy Spirit.

Give it a chance! At first someone praying in tongues or giving a prophecy will seem strange. When someone rests in the Spirit it may frighten you. Resting in the Spirit is being overpowered by God's love and going into a sleep-like state as the Lord gently heals and touches the person with peace and love.

Afterword

The Great Fifty Days

THIS BOOK has tried to make the Scriptures of the great Fifty Days of Easter come alive. They all lead up to Pentecost. Now our task is to live the mystery and reality of Pentecost by inviting the Holy Spirit to overpower us. Let us continue to pray with Pope John that the new Pentecost will be real in all of our lives, and let us thank the Lord for the gift of the Charismatic Renewal that has brought so many to the Holy Spirit.

With Pope John XXIII we pray:

"Renew your wonders in this our day as by a New Pentecost. Grant to your Church that, being of one mind and steadfast in prayer with Mary, Mother of Jesus and following the lead of blessed Peter, it may advance the reign of our Divine Saviour, the reign of truth and justice, the reign of love and peace. Amen."

Alleluia! Alleluia! Alleluia!

Recommended Reading

Aridas, Rev. Chris and John J. Boucher. *Bringing Prayer Meetings to Life.* Pecos, NM: Dove Publications, 1990.

Boucher, John and Therese. *An Introduction to the Catholic Charismatic Renewal.* Ann Arbor, MI: Servant Publications, 1994.

Boucher, Therese. *New Life in the Spirit Seminars: Catholic Edition 2000.* South Bend, IN: Chariscenter USA, 2000.

Charismatic Renewal Services, 237 N. Michigan St., South Bend, IN 46601. 800-348-2227. CRS is the largest distributor of charismatic books, tapes and music in the United States.

Clark, Steve. *Baptized in the Spirit and the Spiritual Gifts.* Ann Arbor, MI: Servant Publications, 1976.

Cordes, Paul Josef. *Call to Holiness: Reflections on the Catholic Charismatic Renewal.* Collegeville, MN: The Liturgical Press, 1997.

DeGrandis, Rev. Robert. *Introduction to the Catholic Charismatic Renewal, Growth in the Spirit, The Gift of Tongues.* HOM Books, 108 Aberdeen St., Lowell, MA 01850.

Mansfield, Patti Gallagher. *As By a New Pentecost: The Dramatic Beginnings of the Catholic Charismatic Renewal.* Steubenville, OH: Franciscan University Press, 1992.

Martin, Rev. Francis. *Baptism in the Holy Spirit: A Scriptural Foundation.* Steubenville, OH: Franciscan University Press, 1986.

McDonnell, Kilian and George T. Montague, ed., *Fanning the Flame: What Does Baptism in the Holy Spirit Have to Do with Christian Initiation?* Collegeville, MN: Liturgical Press, 1991.

Pastoral Statement on the Catholic Charismatic Renewal (1984) and *Grace for the New Springtime,* (1997). USCC

Catholic Conference, 1312 Massachusetts Ave., N.W. Washington, DC 20005-4105.

Pentecost Today Newsletter. Editor, Ron Ryan. P.O. Box 628, Locust Grove, VA 22508-0628. Published monthly, the newsletter is free of charge.

Schubert, Linda. *Miracle Hour* and *5-Minute Miracles.* Miracles of the Heart Ministries, P.O. Box 4034, Santa Clara, CA 95056, 1991.

Walsh, Vincent M. *Key to the Charismatic Renewal in the Catholic Church.* Wynnewood, PA: Key of David Publications, 1974.

Published by Resurrection Press

For a free catalog call 1-800-892-6657